LIVE IN RELATIONSHIP
Sex and Beyond

LIVE IN RELATIONSHIP
Sex and Beyond

Viveck Mathuur

KALPAZ

Live in Relationship (Sex and Beyond)

ISBN: 978-81-7835-913-7

Published in 2012 in India by
Kalpaz Publications
C-30, Satyawati Nagar,
Delhi-110052
E-mail: kalpaz@hotmail.com
Phone : 9212729499

Lasser Type Setting : Quick Media, Delhi
Printed at : Chawla Offset Printers, Delhi

Dedication

"To My Ex-Bosses couple, Mr. Dhawan (A Bachelor) and Ms. Ghosh (A divorcee), who have 'Lived-in' together for more than Thirty Years and have stood by each other in every thick and thin of the circumstances inspiring me to highlight the Global Issue of Live-in-Relationships."

VIVECK MATHUUR

Contents

Preface

"Give neither advice nor salt, until you are asked for it." - *English proverb.*

Live-in Relationship – Sex and Beyond is not intended to advocate people wether to accept or not the 'live-in relationship' as their lifestyle. It is simply a peep into the privacy of individuals, who have now openly come up with their views for or against the fundamentals of cohabitation.

Human relationships are complex and fragile. Sometimes, after seeing each other exclusively for a while, they talk about the possibility of co-habitating or living together before even contemplating marriage.

India's original name, Bharat, is derived from the name of the son born of the union between Shakuntala (adopted daughter of Sage Kanva) and King Dushyanta, born out of wedlock. Shakuntala herself was born out of wedlock through the union of Sage Vishwamitra and the beautiful '*Apsara*' (celestial female dancer) Menaka. In the Mahabharata, Kunti, the mother of the Pandava brothers, begot a son before marriage, born out of her union with Surya, the Sun God. Even after her marriage to Pandu, three out of the five Pandavas were sired by gods who were not her husbands. These two illustrations from the *Mahabharata* underscore that both pre-marital sex and sex after marriage with another man was a fact.

Of course there are those who are happy to consensually and permanently enter into a live-in relationship without having there any expectations of marriage. But most couples agree to live together hoping to base their decision about whether or not to get married, on the outcome of the live-in relationship.

Live-in relation *i.e.* Cohabitation is an arrangement whereby two people decide to live together on a long term or permanent basis in an emotionally and/or sexually intimated relationship. The term is most frequently applied to couples who are not married.

Why is it that, there are some couples ready to leap into marriage while there are others who would like to go through a "trial period" before committing themselves to marriage?

The reason most couples give for living together is, to check their "Compatibility Quotient". Others do it because it is convenient; they are anyhow spending most of their time in each other's homes, so why not conserve time and energy? Some have even decided to marry and live together in the engagement period, as it cuts their expenses and works out better economically. A small percentage of couples lives together, because most of their friends are in live-in relationships and they don't want to be considered as the odd ones out. And in yet others, there is a basic, deep-rooted fear of a lifelong commitment like marriage, either because they have been hurt in the past or are offspring of traumatic divorces.

India is a country, which is slowly opening its doors to the Western ideas and lifestyles, and one of the most controversial episodes amongst it, is the concept of live-in relationships. We can witness the number of unmarried partners living together is scaling high day by day. Just a generation or two ago, it was scandalous for an unmarried man and woman to live together as couple. Today, most couples, who marry, live together first and this has become a trend. But that change happened so quickly, it is no wonder things are inconsistent.

Some couples find convenient living together. Others find themselves attacked by angry family members, excluded from faith communities baffled by how to introduce each other and discriminated because because of not being married. In some places and situations, unmarried partners can share a policy and get certain legal protections; in other situations they are considered legal strangers with no rights, even if they have lived together for decades.

Whenever we think about live-in relationships, the question raises that why do couples believe in having such a relationship, and then there are many answers emerged to it. Researches shows that most couples who live together would like to get married someday, and within five years, slightly more than half of them definitely also do that Couples move in together, mainly because of being in love and they want to spend more time together. They also want to make sure they are compatible, before they make a lifetime commitment to each other. Many people we talk to say they could not imagine marrying someone if they had not lived together first.

Some couples who are engaged and soon to be married also decide to live together before the wedding, since they want to save money for their wedding and they are spending most nights together anyway and don't want to pay two rents, as they are living separate.

However, some couples also might live-in together if they decide not to get married or they figure out that in due course they cannot marry each other. They also know their partner is not a good match for a long-term relationship, but want to stick with the person for obvious reasons. They would also lose significant financial benefits, if they were to marry. This predicament is especially common among senior citizens (who would sometimes lose a pension from a deceased spouse if they married) and disabled people.

Some couples, who live together, do not want to get married, and some (like gay and lesbian couples) are prevented from marrying.

These studies receive a great deal of publicity because conservative groups use them to try to revive "traditional" marriage (with no cohabitation and no sex before marriage). Rather than trying to scare people away from living together when it's already so wide spread, it is important to help the couples living together to have strong and healthy relationships. Married people may be happier on average, but this may be the result of some other factor - it may not be marriage that makes them happier.

Apart from the reasons of a live-in relationship, people feel that couples, who live together before marriage, are more likely to divorce. However by these studies' conclusions are frequently misrepresented in the media. Most couples today live together before they marry, and research shows that on average, the minority of couples who marry without living together tend to be more religious, more conservative, and more opposed to divorce, as one would expect.

So these studies actually show, that people who are more opposed to divorce, are less likely to divorce - which is not particularly surprising. Researchers have found that when you "control" for the differences between the two groups, the cohabitation-divorce link decreases considerably or vanishes entirely, depending on the study. The idea that living together ruins relationships is not supported in any research.

However, even live-in relationships come under the scrutiny of the moral brigade, leaving very little options left to the couples actually staying together. So will this continue or is there an end to such questions and expectations from the older generations?

Like everything coming from the West, live-in relationships are also considered cool and hit in our young society, so much so that couples these days prefer to live with their partners for some time before finally settling for marriage. Even the government has been forced to have consideration of such relationships. The recent changes in the law against domestic violence promises equal benefits to women involved in such relationships for "reasonable long period", the status of wives. But like everything else, it also has both pros and cons. Legalising "live-in relationships" has generated a fierce debate across the society with a section hailing it as a pragmatic move, while others fearing that it will destroy the sanctity of marriage.

In terms of legal practices, how to define what a live-in relation is? Who will decide that it's actually a live-in relation? Is it enough that one guy and one girl stays together in one flat without any paperwork or bond, it's a legal live-in relationship? Or you need to have sex at least once so as to conform it as legal? What? The complexities of this bill are more then what we can think... Wonder how many people actually opt for a 'without marriage', 'without compulsion' lifestyle in India?

In some jurisdictions cohabitation can be viewed legally as common-law marriages, either after the duration of a specified period, or the birth of the couple's child, or if the couple consider and behave accordingly as husband and wife. (This helps provide the surviving partner, a legal basis for inheriting the deceased's belongings in the event of the death of their cohabiting partner.)

With the Supreme Court of India declaring that the right to live together is part of the right to life, it has become necessary to look at the legal rights and obligations for live-in couples around the world also. While heterosexual couples who are in a live-in relationship are called "co-habitant", same sex couples are legally defined as "civil partners". But the law on cohabitation rights is largely evolving and many participants are still unaware of their rights and duties to each other.

All said and done, living together without marriage is a big decision, and it should not to be taken lightly. It has long-term repercussions on the relationship, so it's worth weighing the advantages and disadvantages and "looking before you leap".

In this book we have collected the views and ideas of the people from different walks of life and have varied views, agreements and disagreements on this kind of relationship. We have tried to be impartial while collecting the ideas and thoughts from the masses and have avoided imposing our views and have left it for the readers to decide after considering the good and bad of whether to live in this kind of relationship is pertinent, advisable and right or not.

The ideas from all over the world including the societies other than Indian are also been chosen at random as received thru emails. The views of the contributors have been included, before and after the legalising of Cohabitation by the Supreme Court of India.

The book is mainly based on the Agreeing and Disagreeing people, who have put forward their points of view and have come out with their respective ideas in opposition or support of the 'Concept of Cohabiting' or 'Living-in'. Whatever one may say, in this era of globalisation, amalgamation of different cultures and traditions is inevitable. The argument for and against the issue of live-in relationship will continue for a long time.

Viveck Mathuur

1
Understanding Live-In Together or Cohabitation

In technical terms, live-in together means An arrangement whereby two people decide to live or dwell together on a long term or permanent basis as husband and wife, in an emotionally as well as sexually, personally and closely acquainted connection or in other words **Intimate Relationship**. The **Marriage** between the two persons has not actually taken place. Hence, the act of living together and having a sexual relationship especially without being married or the state or condition of living together as husband and wife without being legally married is Cohabitation or a state of 'Live-in Relationship'.

Before proceeding further with the main subject of Living-in, we must first understand what 'Intimate Relationship' and 'Marriage' actually mean.

What is an Intimate Relationship?

An **intimate relationship** can particularly be defined by these characteristics: enduring behavioural inter-dependence, repeated interactions, emotional attachment, and need fulfillment.

Human being have a universal need to love, which is satisfied, when an intimate relationship is formed. Intimate relationships consist of the people that we are attracted to, whom we like, love and adore emotionally and sexually. Physical intimacy is characterised by romantic or passionate love and attachment, or sexual activity. Such intimate relationships provide people with a social network of a community that provide strong emotional affection and fulfill our universal needs of belongingness and the need to be cared for.

The in-depth study of intimate relationships is a relatively new area of research that has emerged within the last few decades. Although this in-depth and systematic study of intimate relationships is fairly recent, but social thought and analysis of intimate relationships dates back to early Greek philosophers.

What is Marriage?

Marriage is to unite in matrimony and to take a person for husband or wife. It is a social union or legal contract between individuals that creates a relationship. It is an institution, foundation or an establishment in which interpersonal relationships, usually intimate and sexual, are acknowledged in a variety of ways, depending on the culture, subculture or civilisation in which it is found. Such a union is called *matrimony*.

People marry for many reasons, most often including one or more of the following: legal, social, emotional, economical, spiritual, religious and sexual. The reasons may also include family obligations, the legal establishment of a nuclear family unit, the legal protection of children and public declaration of love and affection. Almost all cultures that recognise marriage also recognise adultery as a violation of the terms of marriage.

What is A 'Live-in Relationship'?

Today, cohabitation is a common pattern among people in the Western world. People may live together for a number of reasons. These may include the need to check compatibility or to establish financial security before marrying. It may be also because they are unable to marry legally, for example same-sex, some inter-racial or inter-religious marriages are not permitted and illigal too. Other reasons include living with someone before marriage in an effort to avoid divorce, a way for polygamists to avoid breaking the law, a way to avoid the higher income taxes paid by some two-income married couples (in the United States), negative effects on pension payments (among older people), and philosophical opposition to the *institution of marriage* and seeing little difference between the commitment to live together and the commitment to marriage. Some individuals also may choose cohabitation because they see their relationships as being private and personal matters, and not to be controlled by political, religious or patriarchal institutions.

Some couples prefer cohabitation because it does not legally commit them for an extended period, and because it is easier to establish and dissolve without the legal costs often associated with a divorce. In some jurisdictions cohabitation can be viewed legally as common-law marriage, either after the duration of a specified period, or after the birth of the couple's child, or if the couple consider and behave accordingly as husband and wife. So, living together without getting married can be truly defined as a "Live-in Relationship".

"It's better to have a live-in relationship rather than having a divorced life!" This is common and quite rational line favoring live-in relations in the world. Live-in relationships are not new concept for Western countries, but these days this is adjusting its roots in east also. The word live-in is controversial in many terms in Eastern countries. But the present generation is very much influenced with this concept, in the whole world. The legal definition of live-in relationship is "an arrangement of living under which the couples who are unmarried lives together and enjoy varied benefits of the companionship".

The basic idea of cohabitation or conducting a live-in relationship is that the interested couple wanted to test their compatibility for each other before going for some commitment; the other reasons are some financial concerns or homosexuality. In some parts of world these types of relationships are valid, but some countries are highly strict for not to accepting this concept. It has been found that the younger generation is wider to accept the live-in relationships.

Why Live-in?

This is a general question which can strike at anybody's mind that when arrangement of marriage is for two persons in love is here, then why couples are leaning towards the live-in relationships. This question can have multiple answers, but this have been found that almost all the couples persuing a live-in relation are willing to get married someday. But before that, they want to spend some time with one another, for understanding each other and to figure out their compatibility. Because they believe that if they found themselves incompatible after marriage then they will have no choice other than compromising with their lifestyles.

Some couples believe that opting to get married is just a wastage of money and time, because they think their love doesn't need a legal paper certification or social drama. The reasons can be numerous, depending upon different mental set-ups.

Need of the Modern World

Today, many traditional communities are heading up in the world who opposes live-in relationships and they found it against their religious concerns and social foundations. But it has to be understood that the emotional bindings and relationships can never be pressed by power. Live-in concept is not a Social Problem; it is just a Social Thought. And it has to be entertained rationally. If today's youth is getting more influenced with the concept, then ethical and legal communities of world must take some necessary steps to keep the concept original and rational. In spite of threatening people about live-in relationships, they should support and help the couples who are living together so that one day they could go for some healthier and more social relationship.

Conclusion

It is generally felt that "live-in couples" are move likely to divorce each other. But that is not true. Reports have been shown, that the live-in couples are more opposite to divorce then married ones because of their social or religious concerns. It's quite rational also because most of couples go for live-in relations because they hate to be divorced, so why they will do the same after marriage?

Well, still the opposing communities are on the rock, and it is uncertain that the live-in concept is acceptable or not? But it is rooting up day by day and it needs ethical and legal concerns.

Region wise Popularity

The popularity of cohabitation can be seen region wise as below:

America

- In Mexico, 18.7 percent of couples were cohabiting as of 2005. *Ley de sociedad de convivencia*: the Spanish name for "Cohabitation Societies Law", legislation created on November 9, 2006, by the Legislation Assembly of Mexico City to establish legal rights and duties for all those cases where two people (due to either sexual, familial or friendly reasons) are living together.
- In Canada, 16 percent of couples were cohabiting as of 2001 (29.8 percent in Quebec, and 11.7 percent in the other provinces).
- **Cohabitation in the United States** became common in the late 20th century. Seven states still have anti-cohabitation laws on the books, but they are almost never enforced and are now believed to be unconstitutional since the legal decision Lawrence vs. Texas in 2003.

COHABITATION IN THE UNITED STATES

Statistics

Cohabitation was illegal in all states prior in 1970, but went on to gain status as a common law, subject to certain requirements. Then, the American legal history was witnessed to several sex legislations, which paved the way for living together contracts and their cousins, the "pre-nuptial agreements". The country later institutionalised cohabitation by giving to cohabiters essentially the same rights and obligations as married couples, a situation similar to Sweden and Denmark. Those living together are not recognised as legal parents.

In most parts of the United States, there is no legal registration or definition of cohabitation, so demographers have developed various methods of identifying cohabitation and measuring its prevalence. Most important of these is the Census Bureau, which currently describes an "unmarried partner" as "A person aged 15 years and over, who is not related to the householder, who shares living quarters, and who has a close personal relationship with the householder". Before 1995, the Bureau euphemistically identified any "unrelated" opposite-sex couple living with no other adults as Persons of Same Sex Sharing Living Quarters (POSSLQs), or Persons of Opposite Sex Sharing Living Quarters., and they still report these numbers to show historical trends. However, such measures should be taken loosely, as research says that cohabitation often does not have clear start and end dates, as people move in and out of each other's homes and sometimes do not agree on the definition of their living arrangement at a particular moment.

In the United States 8.2 percent of couples were calculated in 2001 to be cohabiting, majority of them were in the West Coast and New England/Northeastern United States areas.

In 2005, the U.S. Census Bureau reported 4.85 million cohabiting couples, up more than ten times from 1960, when there were 439,000 such couples. The 2002 National Survey of Family Growth found that more than half of all women aged 15 to 44 have lived with an unmarried partner, and that 65 percent of American couples who did cohabitate got married within 5 years.

The cohabiting population is inclusive of all ages, but the average cohabiting age group is between 25 to 34 years.

Stability

A study was made of pre-marital cohabitation of women who are in a monogamous relationship. The study showed "women who are committed to one relationship, who have both pre-marital sex and cohabit only with the man they eventually marry, have no higher incidence of divorce than women who abstain from pre-marital sex and cohabitation. For women in this category, pre-marital sex and cohabitation with their eventual husband are just two more steps in developing a committed, long-term relationship". Teachman's findings report states that "It is only women who have more than one intimate pre-marital relationship who have an elevated risk of marital disruption. This effect is strongest for women who have multiple pre-marital co-residential unions".

Some people have claimed that those who live together before marriage can report having less satisfying marriages and have a higher chance of separating. A possible explanation for this trend could be that people who cohabit prior to marriage did so because of apprehension towards commitment, and when, following marriage, marital problems arose (or, for that matter, before marriage, when relationship problems arose during the cohabitation arrangement), this apprehension was more likely to translate into an eventual separation. It should be noted this model cites antecedent apprehension concerning commitment as the cause of increased break ups and cohabitation only as an indicator of such apprehension. Another explanation is that those who choose not to cohabit prior to marriage are often more conservative in their religious views and may hold more traditional views on gender roles, a mindset that might prevent them from divorcing for religious reasons or confronting crisis in relationships despite experiencing marital problems no less severe than those encountered by former cohabitants. In addition, the very act of living together may lead to attitudes that make happy marriages more difficult. The findings of one recent study, for example, suggest "there may be less motivation for cohabiting partners to develop their conflict resolution and support skills". (One important exception: cohabiting couples who are already planning to marry each other in the near future have just as good a chance at staying together as couples who don't live together before marriage).

A 2001 study indicated that people who cohabited experienced a divorce rate 50 percent higher after marriage than those who did not, though this may be correlation and not cause-and-effect.

Legal status

Some places, including the state of California, have law that recognise cohabiting couples as **"domestic partners"**. In California, such couples are defined as people who have chosen to share one another's lives in an intimate and committed relationship of mutual caring", including having a "common residence, and are the same sex or persons of opposite sex, if one or both of the persons are over the age of 62". This recognition led to the creation of a Domestic Partners Registry, granting them limited legal recognition and some rights similar to married couples.

Half a century ago, it was illegal in every state for adult lovers to live together without being married. Today, on the other hand, just five states (Mississippi, Virginia, West Virginia, Florida, and Michigan) still criminalise cohabitation by opposite-sex couples, although anti-cohabitation law is generally not enforced. Many legal scholars believe that in light of in *Lawrence vs. Texas,* such laws making cohabitation illegal are unconstitutional (North Carolina Superior Court judge Benjamin Alford struck down the North Carolina law on that basis).

The charge of "unlawful cohabitation" was used in the late nineteenth century to enforce the Edmunds Act, and other federal anti-polygamy laws against the Mormons in the Utah Territory, imprisoning more than 1,300 men. However, incidents of cohabitation by non-polygamists were not charged in that territory at that time. Some modern scholarship suggests the Edmunds Act may be unconstitutional for being in violation of the Free Exercise Clause, although the Supreme Court has repeatedly ruled that neutral laws that happen to impinge on some religious practices are constitutional.

Canada: Living together is legally recognised as "common law marriage" in Canada. In many cases common law couples have the same rights as married couples under the federal law of the country. A common law relationship gets legal sanctity if the couple has been living in a conjugal relationship for at least 12 continuous months, or the couple is parents of a child by birth or adoption, or one of the couple has custody and control of the child and the child is totally dependent on that person for support.

What is Domestic Partnership?

A **domestic partnership** is a legal or personal relationship between two individuals who live together and share a common domestic life but are neither joined by marriage nor a civil union. However, in some jurisdictions, such as Australia, New Zealand, the United States of Oregon, Washington, Nevada, and California, a domestic partnership is almost equivalent to marriage, or to other legally recognized same-sex or different-sex unions. The terminology for such unions is still evolving, and the exact level of rights and responsibilities conferred by a domestic partnership varies widely from place to place.

Some legislatures have voluntarily established domestic partnership relations by statute instead of being ordered to do so by a court. Although some jurisdictions have instituted domestic partnerships as a way to recognise same-sex unions, domestic partnerships may involve either different-sex or same-sex couples.

In some legal jurisdictions, **domestic partners** who live together for an extended period of time but are not legally entitled to common-law marriage may be entitled to legal protection in the form of a domestic partnership. Some domestic partners may enter into **domestic partnership agreements** in order to agree contractually to issues involving property ownership, support obligations, and similar issues common to marriage.

One of the purposes of domestic partnership relation is to recognise the contribution of one partner to the property of the other. In the common law, devices such as the constructive trust are available to protect spouses in legal or common-law marriages. In civil law jurisdictions, such trusts are generally not available, prompting courts to find alternative ways to protect the partner who contributes to the other's property.

Asia

- In Indonesia, an Islamic penal code proposed in 2005 to made cohabitation punishable by up to two years in prison.
- In Japan, according to M. Iwasawa at the National Institute of Population and Social Security Research, less than 3 percent of females between the ages 25 to 29 years are currently cohabiting, but more than 1 in 5 have had some experience of an unmarried partnership, including cohabitation. A more recent Iwasawa study has shown that there has been a recent emergence of non-marital cohabitation. Couples born in the 1950s cohort showed an incidence of cohabitation of 11.8 percent, where the 1960s and 1970s cohorts showed cohabitation rates of 30 percent, and 53.9 percent respectively. The split between urban and rural residence for people who had cohabited is indicates 68.8 percent were urban and 31.2 percent were rural.

- In Bangladesh cohabitation after divorce is frequently punished by the Salishi system of informal courts, especially in rural areas.
- In the Philippines, around 2.4 million Filipinos were cohabiting as of 2004. The year 2000 census placed the percentage of cohabiting couples at 19 percent. The majority of individuals are between the ages of 20-24 and Poverty was often the main factor in decision to cohabit.
- In India, cohabitation had been taboo since British rule. However, this is no longer true in big cities, but is still often found in rural areas with more conservative values. Female live-in partners have economic rights under **Protection of Women from Domestic Violence Act 2005**.

The Maharashtra Government in October, 2008 approved a proposal suggesting a woman involved in such a relationship for a 'reasonable period' should get status of a wife.

The National Commission for women recommended to ministry of women and child development on June 30, 2008 that definition of wife as described in Section 125 of the Criminal Procedure Code, which deals in maintenance, suggested that it include women who are involved in a live-in relationship. Aim of the recommendation was to harmonising other sections of law with protection of women from Domestic Violence. Act that a live-in couple's relationship on a par with that between a legally married husband and wife.

The move has come after Justice Malimath Committee recommended that all states turn into this law. The committee observed that "if man and woman are living together as husband and wife for a reasonable long period, the man shall be deemed to have married the woman".

The Malimath Committee had also suggested that the word 'wife' under Criminal Procedure Code be amended to include a 'woman living with the man like his wife' which means the woman would also be entitled to alimony.

In Payal Katara vs. Superintendent Nari Niketan Kandri Vihar, Agra and Others AIR 2002, the Allahabad High Court ruled out that "a lady of about 21 years of age being a major, has right to go anywhere and that anyone - man and woman even without getting married can live together if they wish".

In Patel and others case, the Apex Court observed that live-in relation between two adults without formal marriage cannot be considered as an offence.

In Abhijit Bhikaseth Auti vs. State Of Maharashtra and Others on 16.09.2009, the Supreme Court also observed that it is not necessary for woman to strictly establish the marriage to claim maintenance under Section 125 of Criminal Procedure Code, a woman living in relationship may also claim maintenance under the same Section.

In Radhika vs. State of Madhya Pradesh AIR 2008, the Supreme Court observed that if a man and woman are involved in live-in relationship for a long period, then they will be treated as a married couple and their child would be called legitimate.

What does Protection of Women from Domestic Violence Act 2005 say?

The **Protection of Women from Domestic Violence Act 2005** was brought into force by the Indian government from October 26, 2006. The Act was passed by the Parliament of India in August 2005 and assented to by the President on 13 September, 2005. As of November 2007, it has been ratified by four of twenty-eight State Governments in India; namely Andhra Pradesh, Tamil Nadu, Uttar Pradesh and Orissa. Of about 8,000 criminal cases registered all over India under this Act, Rajasthan had 3440 cases; Kerala had 1028 while Punjab had 172 cases registered.

Definition

Domestic Violence 1) For the purposes of this Act, any conduct of the respondent shall constitute domestic violence if he (the man), - (a) habitually assaults or makes the life of the aggrieved person miserable by cruelty of conduct even if such conduct does not amount to physical ill-treatment; or (b) forces the aggrieved person to lead an immoral life; or (c) otherwise injures or harms the aggrieved person. (2) Nothing contained in clause (c) of sub-section (1) shall amount to domestic violence if the pursuit of course of conduct by the respondent was reasonable for their own protection or for the protection of their or another's property.

Scope

Primarily meant to provide protection to the wife or female live-in partner from domestic violence at the hands of the husband or male live-in partner or his relatives, the law also extends its protection to women who are sisters, widows or mothers.

The salient features of the Protection from Domestic Violence Act, 2005 are as follows:

- The Act seeks to cover those women who are or have been in a relationship with the abuser where both parties have lived together in a shared household and are related by consanguinity (relationship by blood), marriage or a relationship in the nature of marriage, or adoption; in addition relationship with family members living together as a joint family are also included. Even those women who are sisters, widows, mothers, single women, or living with the abuser are entitled to get legal protection under the proposed Act.
- "Domestic violence" includes actual abuse or the threat of abuse that is physical, sexual, verbal, emotional and economic. Harassment by way of unlawful dowry demands to the woman or her relatives would also be covered under this definition.

- One of the most important features of the Act is the woman's right to secure housing. The Act provides for the woman's right to reside in the matrimonial or shared household, whether or not she has any title or rights in the household. This right is secured by a residence order, which is passed by a court. These residence orders cannot be passed against anyone who is a woman.
- The other relief envisaged under the Act is that of the power of the court to pass protection orders that prevent the abuser from aiding or committing an act of domestic violence or any other specified act, entering a workplace or any other place frequented by the abused, attempting to communicate with the abused, isolating any assets used by both the parties and causing violence to the abused, her relatives and others who provide her assistance from the domestic violence.
- The draft Act provides for appointment of Protection Officers and **NGOs** (Non-Governmental Organizations) to provide assistance to the woman with respect to medical examination, legal aid, safe shelter, etc.
- The Act provides for breach of protection order or interim protection order by the respondent as a cognisable and non-bailable offence punishable with imprisonment for a term which may extend to one year or with fine which may extend to twenty thousand rupees or with both. Similarly, non-compliance or discharge of duties by the Protection Officer is also sought to be made an offence under the Act with similar punishment.

While "economic abuse" includes deprivation of all or any economic or financial resources to which the victim is entitled under any law or custom whether payable under an order of a Court or otherwise or which the victim requires out of necessity including, but not limited to, household necessities for the aggrieved person and her children, if any, 'Stridhan' (money as received by the woman at various functions / occasions during her life time, fully recognised by the Indian Law), property, jointly or separately owned by her, payment of rental related to the shared household and maintenance and disposal of household effects, any alienation of assets whether movable or immovable, valuables, shares, securities, bonds and the like or other property in which the victim has an interest or is entitled to use by virtue of the domestic relationship or which may be reasonably required by the victim or her children or her 'Stridhan' or any other property jointly or separately held by the victim and prohibition or restriction to continued access to resources or facilities which the victim is entitled to use or enjoy by virtue of the domestic relationship including access to the shared household, "physical abuse" means any act or conduct which is of such a nature as to cause bodily pain, harm or danger to life, limb, or health or impair the health or development of the victim and includes assault, criminal intimidation and criminal force.

Criticism

Men's organisations such as **Save Indian Family** and **Save Family Foundation** have criticised the law since it is not gender neutral and abused men are not covered. Moreover, it might be abused by women and their families during family disputes. The Indian Minister for Women and Child Development in the UPA Government, Ms. Renuka Chowdhury had said that "an equal gender law would be ideal. But there is simply too much physical evidence to prove that it is mainly the woman who suffers at the hands of man". In an Interview given to an English News Channel, she commented that "this act won't hit good hubbies". The former Attorney General of India Soli Sorabjee has also criticised the broad definition of verbal abuse in the Act. The President of India, Ms. Pratibha Devisingh Patil, in one of her speeches had mentioned that another disquieting trend has been that women themselves have not been innocent of abusing women.

At times women have played an unsavory, catalytic role in perpetrating violence whether against the daughter-in-law, the mother-in-law or female domestic helps. Instances exist whereby protective legal provisions for the benefit of women have been subjected to distortion and misuse to wreak petty vengeance and to settle scores. Some surveys have concluded that around 80 percent of dowry complaints are false and were registered primarily to settle scores. It is unfortunate if laws meant to protect women get abused as instruments of oppression.

Europe

- In late 2005, 21 percent of families in Finland consisted of cohabitating couples (all age groups). Of couples with children, 18 percent were cohabitating. Of ages 18 and above in 2003, 13.4 percent were cohabitating. Generally, cohabitation amongst Finns is most common for people under 30. Legal obstacles for cohabitation were removed in 1926 in a reform of the Finnish penal code, while the phenomenon was socially accepted much later on among non-Christian Finns.
- In Denmark, Norway and Sweden, cohabitation is very common; roughly 50 percent of all children are born into families of unmarried couples, whereas the same figure for several other Western European countries is roughly 10 percent. Many couples decide to marry later.
- In the UK, 25 percent of children are now born to cohabiting parents.
- In Bulgaria, cohabitation is very common; 53.4 percent of all children born in the year 2009 were into families of unmarried couples.
- In France, 17.5 percent of couples were cohabiting as of 1999.

Scotland: Family law (Scotland) Act 2006, for the first time identified, and in the process by default legalised, live-in relationships of over 150000 cohabiting couples in the country. Section 25 (2) of the Act said that a court of law can consider a person as a cohabitant of another by checking on three factors; the length of the period during which they lived together, the nature of the relationship during that period and the nature and extent of any financial arrangements.

In case of breakdown of relationship, under section 28, a cohabitant has the right to apply in court for financial support. This is in case of separation and not death of either partner. If a partner dies intestate, the survivor can move the court for financial support from his estate. However, all these remedies will be applicable only if a person moves court within six months from the death of his live-in partner.

France: Live in relationships are governed by the Civil Solidarity Pact of *'pacte civil de solidarite'* or PaCS, passed by the French National Assembly in October 1999. Cohabitation is defined as a "de facto stable and continuous relationship" between two persons of different sexes or of the same sex living together as couple. The pact defines the relationship as a contract, and the couples involved as "contractants". The contract binds "two adults of different sexes or of the same sex, in order to organise their common life" For a valid contract to exist, the contractants "may not be bound" by another pact, "by marriage, sibling or lineage".

United Kingdom: Live-in relationships are largely covered by the Civil Partnership Act 2004.Though a man and woman living together in a stable sexual relationship are often referred to as "common law spouses", the expression is not wholly correct in law in England and Wales. The United Kingdom feels that live in partners owe each other more than that to be worthy of the term. As per a 2010 note from the Home Affairs Section to the House of Commons, unmarried couples have no guaranteed rights to ownership of each other's property on breakdown of relationship. If a cohabiting couple separates, the courts have no power to override the strict legal ownership of each other's property on breakdown of relationship. If a cohabiting couple separates, the courts have no power to override the strict legal ownership of property and divide it as they may do on divorce. In cases of domestic violence, cohabitants can benefit from the provisions of the Family Law Act, 1996 which allows "home sharers and former home sharers (including some sex partners) to apply for non-molestation orders and / or court orders regulating the occupation of the family home".

Unmarried partners have no automatic inheritance over their partner's assets on death. Cohabiting couples are treated as unconnected individuals for taxation purposes. The list of persons eligible to register a death does not automatically include a cohabitant. The best way to be safe for live-in couples is to "enter into a cohabitation agreement and this can act as encouragement for them to consider what they would want to happen if the relationship ends". But the Government is still not very confident. "Cohabitation agreements have yet to be fully tested in court and so it is not entirely clear what weight will be given to them", says the note.

London, March 26, 2010 - The Office for National Statistics has revealed that couples who are married are less likely to split up than those who live together. Analysis of Census results found that four-fifths of spouses who were married in 1991 were still together a decade later, compared with three-fifths of cohabiting couples.

The independent statistics body said older couples and those with children were more likely to stay in the same relationships.

The findings of the Office for National Statistics are likely to reignite the political debate over whether married couples should be given tax breaks.

The Conservatives have pledged to recognise marriage in the tax system, ensuring that spouses would not lose out if one wanted to stay at home to raise their children, on the grounds that stable families are good for society.

But labour ministers, who abolished tax breaks for married couples, say that families now come in "all shapes and sizes" and so it would be wrong to disadvantage single parents or widows.

The Office for National Statistics report, included in a new edition of its regular publication, Population Trends, analysed the information about living arrangements provided by 318,533 adults in its own Longitudinal Study.

Researchers tracked those who answered questions in both the 1991 and 2001 Census then looked in detail to find out whether they remained in the same relationship over the decade.

Researchers found that those who were cohabiting in 1991, 61 percent out of them were with the same partner 10 years later, while 39 percent were not.

Those who stayed together, most had married their partner. The majority whose relationship had ended were living alone.

By contrast, 82 percent of those who were married in 1991 were still with their spouse in 2001. Of the 18 percent who had divorced or been widowed, most were single although a small proportion had remarried.

Detailed models suggested that couples were more likely to split up if they were younger, had no children, had previously split up with partners, were poorly educated or were unemployed.

"The Government persists in saying there's no difference between marriage and other forms of relationship, but these official statistics are telling us, from a completely neutral standpoint that there is a difference. Living together is not an equivalent to marriage for family stability. That's why it's important to protect and support marriage, in the interests of children", Jill Kirby, Director of the Centre for Policy Studies said.

Marriage rates are already at their lowest level since records began in 1862, with just 232,990 weddings took place in England and Wales during 2008.

But despite the greater instability of cohabitation, the Office for National Statistics believes even fewer couples are likely to tie the knot in future.

"There have been notable changes in United Kingdom partnership behaviour over the last 40 years. Divorce rates rose considerably during the 1970s, remained broadly stable after the mid-1980s, and more recently have fallen since 2004. At the same time, there has been a long-term fall in marriage rates since the beginning of the 1970s, and a steady increase in the proportion of adults cohabiting. For unmarried men in Great Britain aged 16 to 59, the proportion cohabiting increased from 11 percent in 1986 to 27 percent in 2007. There was a similar change for equivalent unmarried women, from 13 percent to 28 percent. This change in partnership behaviour is likely to persist." the report said.

"According to demographic projections, the long-term rise in cohabitation will continue, with the number of cohabiting couples in England and Wales projected to rise from 2.25 million in 2007 to 3.70 million in 2031, the same figures show that the proportion of the adult population that is legally married is projected to fall from 49 percent in 2007 to 41 percent by 2031", it concluded.

Ireland: Though living together is legally recognised, news reports from Ireland says the public is up in arms against a new legislation to introduce legal rights for "separated" live-in couples to demand maintenance or share their property with their dependent partners. The scheme will apply to both opposite sexes and same sex unmarried couples, who have been living together for three years, or two years in the case of a cohabiting couple with children. The Government, with this legislation, intends to provide legal and financial protection for vulnerable and financially dependent cohabitants in the event of death or the break-up of a relationship.

Middle East

- The cohabitation rate in Israel is less than 3 percent of all couples, compared to 8 percent, on average, in West European countries.
- Cohabitation is illegal according to **Sharia Law** (for the countries that enforce it).

Before proceeding further we should understand what Sharia Law summarily says

Sharia "way" or "path" refers to the sacred law of Islam. All Muslims believes that Sharia is God's law, but they have differences between themselves as to exactly what it entails. Modernists, traditionalists and fundamentalists all hold different views of Sharia, as do adherents to different schools of Islamic thought and scholarship. Different countries and cultures have varying interpretations of Sharia, as well.

Muslims believes that all Sharia is derived from two primary sources, the divine revelations set forth in the Qur'an, and the sayings and example set by the Islamic Prophet Muhammad in the Sunnah. "Fiqh", or "jurisprudence", interprets and extends the application of Sharia to questions not directly addressed in the primary sources, by including secondary sources. These secondary sources usually include the consensus of the religious scholars embodied in "Ijma", and analogy from the Qur'an and Sunnah through "Qiyas". Shia jurists replace Qiyas analogy with "aql" or "reason". Where it enjoys official status, Sharia is applied by Islamic judges, or "Qazis". The Imam has varying responsibilities depending on the interpretation of Sharia. While the term is commonly used to refer to the leader of communal prayers, the Imam may also be a scholar, religious leader or political leader. Sharia deals with many topics addressed by secular law, including crime, politics and economics, as well as personal matters such as sexuality, hygiene, diet, prayer, and fasting.

Introduction (or reintroduction) of Sharia is a longstanding goal for Islamist movements in Muslim countries. Some Muslim minorities in Asia (e.g. India) have attained institutional recognition of Sharia to adjudicate their personal and community affairs. In Western countries, where Muslim immigration is more recent, Muslim minorities have introduced Sharia family law, for use in their own disputes, with varying degrees of success (e.g. Britain's Muslim Arbitration Tribunal). Attempts to impose Sharia have been accompanied by controversy, violence, and even warfare as in the Second Sudanese Civil War.

Oceania

- In New Zealand, 18.3 percent of couples were cohabiting as of 2001.
- In Australia, 22 percent of couples were cohabiting as of 2005.

Australia: The Family Law Act states that a "de facto relationship" can exist between two people of different or the same sex and that a person can be in a de-facto relationship even if legally married to another person or in a de-facto relationship with someone else.

2
Relationship and Spiritual Life

Maureen Jones, Norway - Intimacy with one woman or one man is much better than having many superficial relationships. Love is not like a seasonal flower, it takes years to grow. And only when it grows it goes beyond biology, and starts having something of the spiritual in it.

Spiritual life is essentially based on love, and our love depends on the character and level of our relationships. Relationships are the great fabric of life. To unfold them consciously and methodically is to learn to love through a work that includes all of life. It is to transform living into an art.

Nevertheless, the term 'spiritual life' is generally associated with a belief, rather than with the task of living. When we refer to 'spiritual life', we need to remember that no one's life is autonomous or isolated. We live in relationship, not only with other persons and our immediate surroundings but with the world, with time and with the mystery of not knowing who we are, where we came from and where we are going. Most especially we need to remember that we live in relationship with the fundamental principle of the Universe, that which we call God or the Divine.

Just being with many women or many men will keep you entertained maybe, but superficial; occupied certainly, but that occupation is not going to help in inward growth. But a one-to-one relationship is a sustained relationship so that you can understand each other more closely, is tremendously beneficial.

When we say that we want to be happy, that we yearn for fulfillment, we are actually expressing the human need to unveil the mystery of the Divine. We know that explanations of life and the world are not enough. We find real fulfillment and happiness only when the Divine becomes part of our self-awareness.

This realisation is traditionally called 'Union with God'. But the traditional definition does not include the fact that we are united with all of reality; we live in a great web of relationships that includes everything. If we were to think of the unfolding of the soul as a process that takes place only between the individual and the Divine, we would separate the human being from reality. Our relationship with others and with the world is not simply an arena where our spiritual transformation takes place. On the contrary, spiritual unfolding becomes possible when it is based on the harmonisation of the relationship that we have with all human beings and with all aspects of life.

Relationship is needed only because you can't be alone, because you are not yet capable of meditation. Hence, meditation is a 'MUST' before you really love. One should be capable of being alone, utterly alone, and yet tremendously blissful. Then you can love. Then your love is no more a need but a sharing, no more a necessity. You will not become dependent on the people you love. You will share - and sharing is beautiful.

Relationship is a thing: you cling to it. Relating is a flow, a movement, a process. You meet a person, you love because you have so much love to give - and the more you give, the more you have. This is just against the economic laws that operate in the outside world. Once you have known that, if you want to have more love and more joy, you give and share.

That is why the idea of relationship is so important to our spiritual realisation. The human being is inseparable from the universe: we are and we live in relationships. Yet our relationship with the world unknown to us; we are aware of only some of our relationships, especially those which we voluntarily choose. But we live in relationship whether we want to or not, whether we realise it or not. Nothing exists apart from us; everything exists along with us - it includes us.

No relationship can satisfy, because every relationship begins with great hope, and that is not possible to be fulfilled. Yes, that hope can be fulfilled, but it can be fulfilled only when you have fallen in love with the whole. A part can't fulfill it. When you have fallen in love with the total, when the merger happens with the total, only then there will be contentment. There will be nobody who is contented, there will be simply contentment. And then there is no end to it.

That's what happens in every relationship. Rather than giving you contentment, it gives you a tremendous discontentment. Each relationship fails in this world - and it is good that it fails; it would have been a curse if it was not so. It is a blessing that it fails. Because each relationship fails, that's why you start searching for the ultimate relationship with God, with existence, with the cosmos. You see the futility again and again, that it is not going to be satisfied by any man, by any woman; that each experience ends in tremendous frustration, begins in great hope and leaves you in great hopelessness. It is always so, it comes with great romance and ends in a bitter taste. When it happens again and again, one has to learn something - that each relationship is only an experimentation to prepare you for the ultimate relationship, for the ultimate love affair.

If you move into a relationship when you are feeling lonely, then you will exploit the other. The other will become a means to satisfy you. You will use the other, and everybody resents being used because no one is here to become a means for anybody else.

Whenever you move in any relationship out of loneliness, the relationship is already on the rocks. Even before it has started, it is already on the rocks. Even before the birth, the child is dead. It is going to create more misery for you. And remember, when you move from your loneliness you will fall in relationship with somebody who is in the same plight, because no man who is really living his aloneness will be attracted towards you. You will be too below him. He can at the most sympathise but cannot love you. One who is on his peak of loneliness can only be attracted towards somebody who is also alone. So whenever you move out of aloneness, you will find a person of the same type; you will find your own reflection somewhere. And remember, when two miserable people meet, it is not an ordinary addition, it is a multiplication. They create much more misery for each other than they could have created in their loneliness.

Out of your unhappiness you seek the other; then the relationship will be wrong. Seek the other out of happiness, and then the relationship will never be wrong. Seek out of happiness. First meditate, first feel your own being, first pray. First grow into love; otherwise what you do when you will find the lover? Then you will never know what to do.

It would be good for those of us who yearn for a better society to look first at our own relationships and to put aside the belief that our originality and authenticity as individuals are expressed in an isolated, fixed or abstract way. This will help us perceive our individuality by the way we relate with the circumstances which actually include and shape who we are.

Whenever you become sexually related, you become afraid, because sex is really not a relationship, it is exploitation. It is an act of escapism. Overall, this relation builds up harmony between the couples, but spoils their social influence. If you attached to a woman or man sexually, you always afraid that this woman may go to somebody else, or this man may move to somebody else. There is no relationship really, it is just mutual exploitation. You are exploiting each other, but you don't love and you know it, so you are afraid.

The spiritual tradition teaches practices that help us accept tolerance, patience, gentleness, compassion. Although these precepts show us the beginning of a basic human relationship, humankind as a whole does not yet live these principles. It is here, at these first steps, that we need to begin to become conscious of the character and level of our relationships in order to understand the task of harmonising and universalising them.

Have a sexual relationship only when you have a loving relationship, so love and sex become associated. And love is a greater centre, a higher centre. Once sex is hitched to love, it starts moving upwards.

Spiritual practices lead to spiritual advancement only when they produce greater harmony in our system of relationships. To imagine that we are unfolding spiritually, while at the same time finding it hard to tolerate, those we live with, would be to distort the meaning of unfolding. Once you feel that you love, never go to pray in a temple or in a mosque or in a church alone. Your first prayer should be with your loved one. Either before you love, pray; or, after you have made love, pray; or - and the third is the best - while you are making love, let there be prayer by you.

Effort is necessary to develop conscious and harmonious relationships. We need interior effort to work on the self-knowledge which will enable us to overcome the idea that we exist separated from others. We also need exterior control so that our conduct does not separate us from others but creates an unbreakable inner tie between ourselves and everyone else.

Relationship is a mirror. Wherever you are related with a person - a wife, a husband, a friend, a lover, an enemy - a mirror is there. The wife mirrors the husband. You can see yourself there, and if you see an ugly husband, don't try to leave your wife - the ugliness is in you. Drop that ugliness! This mirror will show you beautiful, and be thankful to this mirror. But stupid and cowardly people always escape and renounce; brave and wise people continue to live in relationship, and use it as a mirror. Living with someone is a constant mirroring around you. Every moment the other reveals you, exposes you. These relationships are built on honesty, love and forgiveness. The closer the relationship, the clearer is the mirror: the more distant the relationship, the mirror is not so clear.

How we approach one another, how we treat one another, determine the quality of our relationships and of our lifestyle in families, in friendships, in cities, states and nations, in the workplace, in the world. To love and to relate are the same thing; as our relationships become conscious, we become conscious of love. The quality of our relationships shows the nature of that love. As we relate consciously and harmoniously with our reality - which is everything - our love likewise expands and embraces all.

3
Advantages and Disadvantages of a Live-In Relationship

Some of the apparent advantages of a live-in relationship

Whatever the society may feel about the fundamentals of 'Live-In', but it has many pros - it gives a couple (who may be very seriously thinking of spending the rest of their lives together and having a family) an opportunity to get to know the other at various levels, and in different situations.

One gets to know the day-to-day habits and working of the other and then become able to decide if they will be able to deal with those issues for a lifetime or not. Issues of money, running a house, waking and sleeping habits, bed and bathroom etiquettes, are all examined. It may sound trivial but many marriages do end due to the most basic differences including bad sleeping habits (snoring etc.), bathroom habits, sexuality etc.

The freedom and liberty is a liberating factor, by that you choose how you want to live, and with whom, many who are in live-in relationships felt this.

Besides the above, it has many other advantages as well:

1. Economics

You get to share expenses and suddenly all your expenditure is halved. Yet, you can have separate accounts personal. You may not be as accountable to him for how and where you spend, as you may be in a marriage.

2. No messy divorce or legal issues

Since there are no pre-nuptial agreements or marriage contracts, one can walk away without any of the legal hassles that arise from a marriage. On an emotional level, there is no trauma of going through a divorce, it's much easier to love and leave.

3. Testing the waters

If one or both of you need proof that you're right for each other and you manage to coexist smoothly, then you can make an informed decision about marriage.

4. Get to know the realities

When some one is just dating, it's easy for him or her to conceal how messy you are or how much time you take going through your mornings. But once you start living together, you are able to explore every nuance of your significant other's personality, a chance to get acquainted with the real person. You may discover that the partner's nagging really gets to you, and you can't live with it.

5. Companionship

If you're one of those people who feels that the walls close in on you when you're alone, the companionship is constant. You get all the comforts of being married without many of the pitfalls.

A live-in relationship certainly seems to have some advantages over marriage for women, especially with a new study finding that live-in boyfriends do a lot more housework than married men.

The study was carried out by researchers at George Mason University by Theodore Greenstein and Jennifer Gerteisen Marks of North Carolina State University who questioned more than 17,000 people in 28 countries.

They found that married men tend to help around the house less than live-in boyfriends.

According to study co-author, sociologist Shannon Davis, the key finding of the study is that it suggests the institution of marriage changes the division of labour.

Couples with an egalitarian view on gender - seeing men and women as equal - are more likely to divide the household chores equally. However, in married relationships, even if an egalitarian viewpoint is present, men still report doing less housework than their wives.

"Our research suggests that couples across many countries are influenced by similar factors when deciding how to divide the housework. It's the way the society has defined what being married means, the institution itself that affects behaviour. Marriage as an institution seems to have a traditionalising effect on couples - even couples who see men and women as equal." say the researchers.

Some of the disadvantages of a live-in relationship

1. Boredom

However, the pitfalls of living together have also to be considered. Since you've already anticipated most of the pleasures of marriage, when you do decide to get married, there really isn't that much to look forward to.

As a result, a couple can settle into this state of "unwedded bliss" and put off marriage indefinitely. In the event one of the partners is actually holding out for marriage or anticipating a proposal, this could pose a problem.

2. Alienation

Research bears this out by indicating that only a small percentage of those living together actually marry and ironically, there's a high divorce rate among those married that have already lived together.

In case one of the partners or even the parents has a strong religious background which forbids "living in sin", it sets a bad note for the relationship.

3. Breakdown of live-in relationships

Just like every stage of a relationship, living together inevitably runs into its fair share of trouble. Many of the complaints of live-in lovers appear no different from those who are married.

"He doesn't do his fair share of the housework, I shoulder the entire burden."

"She doesn't make the effort to look good like she used to when we were dating."

"We hardly talk anymore."

"He finds time to see his mates but never makes the effort to take me out on a date."

"Sex has become so boring and predictable, not exciting like it used to be!"

"We're always arguing about money."

4. Irresponsibility

So while the complaints are the same, the difference lies in the solution. In a marriage, because of vows taken and the consequences of making a rash decision, people try harder to work through a problem and see it to its logical solution. The price you pay is higher if you don't succeed.

In a live-in relationship, the tolerance levels are much lower and if you don't 'shape up you can ship out'. The difference between the two is the commitment levels. In a live-in relationship, individuals are trying to test whether they can make a go of it; in a marriage they're trying to make it work, no matter what!

The main thing which suffers in this kind of relationship or living arrangement is **Virginity**, so we must understand (technically and according to religion) that what actually Virginity is and what is actually at stake during cohabitation of live-in.

Virginity

Virginity is a term used to describe the state of never having engaged in sexual intercourse. A person who still has his or her virginity can accordingly be described as being a virgin. In broader usage of these terms, they can characterise a state of purity. For example, some cocktails can be described as being "virgin" when they lack alcoholic content. (There is a grade of olive oil called "virgin", as well as a grade called "extra-virgin": the actual definitions are surprising.) Alternatively, it can indicate a lack of experience, such as a player of bingo being described as virgin when he is a newcomer to the game. In other contexts, these terms can apply to someone who has not engaged in sexual activities in general.

With the standard usage of these terms (where the state of purity is thought to come from a lack of sexual intercourse), they have been more commonly applied to women than to men, both historically and in many present-day situations. In fact, the terms traditionally were used to simply describe a unmarried female: It was introduced to English in the 13th century, and via French *virgine* derived from Latin *virgo* (Genitive virginis), which is composed of "*vir*" meaning "man" or "husband", and "*genere*", "created (for)", and already had the meaning of a female in (nuptial) subjection to a male. During the Middle English period, the word "maid" referred to a person, whether male or female, who had never been married or sexually active. Geoffrey Chaucer, for instance, used that word in reference to Christ and St. Paul. However, applying the term to men as well has become uncommon in modern times, as the word "maid" lost currency in reference to men and began to refer only to unmarried women (called maidens) and, later, unmarried domestic servants.

"Are you a virgin?" is still a very shocking question to be asked from a male or a female, particularly when they are grown up enough to get married. It becomes very embarrassing for both to say either 'Yes' or 'No' as both the answers can go against them, depending upon the mentality and thinking of the other. This pithily sums up our attitude towards pre-marital sex.

The 'moral policing' of opposite-sex relationships among the young in India is traced back to age-old restrictions dictated by the implied insistence on virginity in both males and females prior to marriage. When it is present in varied forms from different quarters, youngsters try to carry on clandestinely with their relationships and many suffer from feelings of guilt.

"Sexual intimacy is an important part of the man-woman relationship. It has its own value in bringing people together, making them connect to each other emotionally and physically. It is a form of love and affection that people feel for each other. If two people feel mentally and emotionally ready for this, there is little reason to hold back. All that is important is the awareness of what one is getting into, the reasons for it and the consequences of it. If there is clarity in the mind regarding these aspects, pre-marital sex is just as healthy and fulfilling as post marriage sex. The intention with which a person consents for pre-marital sex is important. A frivolous, rash and casual attitude could appear promiscuous, but an informed and a well-thought out decision would reflect otherwise." says Dr Sanjay Chugh, a Psychiatrist.

"There has been a mass shift in the marriageable age for men and women in cities and metros. Earlier, most people would get married by their early or mid-20s. This age bracket has changed. We now see men and women in their 30s, happily single. Often, this is out of choice. These people have a fair idea of what they want from a relationship and a natural desire to physical and emotional gratification of their needs. In such a scenario, pre-marital sex sounds natural and understandable. Every person has his/her personal sense of morality and value system, based on family teachings and personal experiences. Pre-marital sex would be the individual's own prerogative guided by his own principles and attitude. What is more important is one's mental and emotional readiness for it, as you don't want someone to have an unresolved emotional baggage that complicates matters." Dr. Sanjay Chugh adds.

He sounds an alert by saying "If it's a decision taken mindlessly, as an impulse without thinking of its emotional and social repercussions and without assessing the individual's own preparedness for it, any unpleasantness during the course of the relationship can leave a bad taste in the mouth."

We live in a society which is multicultural. It is not a monolith, nor is it perfect. It is dynamic like life itself, filled with contradictions. Good sex gives a boost to one's self-confidence. Sex is a very private and personal thing. It must remain a personal choice.

There is no fine line one can draw between One Night Stands (ONS) and dating. At one time, the term 'one-night-stand' referred to streetwalkers and call girls picked up by clients for a night instead of a few hours. But now, few believe in dating. "Who wants to be tied down to one guy for ages in a world wide enough for you to surf wildly?" That comes from today's girl.

Dating in urban India is loaded word that suggests ONS mutually entered into by both partners for consensual sex. The boy, 21, and the girl, 18, met at a party. They downed a few pegs of whisky and danced close till they decided to retire together. The "your-place-or-mine" syndrome is so common that youngsters are moving out of their small-town parental shelters to strike it free in an up-market and trendy metropolis.

Another girl opens her heart and says, "I wouldn't dream of seeing anyone except my regular boyfriend in the small town we lived in. It was almost taken for granted that one fine day we would marry and settle down. It took the worry off our respective parents' minds and everything was alright. But I got a fellowship and went to the UK When I came back; I wished to move out to the other town. He did not like it. We had outgrown each other and trying to pretend otherwise would have led to unhappiness. I made my family look at everything from my perspective and finally, it had to relent," says she, who now is a regular one-night-stander.

She says, "It depends solely on how one approaches an ONS relationship. You may call it quits or you may want to see the partner one more time. One thing might lead to another and you find yourself seeing your partner all too often, not necessarily for a backseat-of-the-car session. I would personally never want to marry my ONS partner. I do not think there would be any respect for each other for a lasting relationship based on sheer trust." Dating is democratic. So is an ONS.

Rajesh Ahuja is of the view that most teens feel that ONS is the most lucid and practical relationship one can have as there are no strings attached. Others feel that ONS broadens one's horizons, failing to comment on the well-accepted notion about AIDS being an almost mandatory spin-off of a promiscuous lifestyle. No one feels guilty any more. It is all about experimenting with 'kicks'. If you were a safe-player, you'd choose dating over ONS at the risk of being labelled old-fashioned.

Malini Shah, a youth counsellor, says, "Pre-marital sex is on the rise across all strata, especially in the metros. However, in the middle classes and upper middle classes, these issues are still considered taboo and are done clandestinely. Among the upper middle classes, it is being accepted as a lifestyle trend."

It is time we moved out of the cultural boundaries we have set for ourselves. If a couple like each other and love each other, then physical control should not be a limitation for them.

Physiology

Among females, the hymen is a membrane, part of the vulva, which partially occludes the entrance to the vagina and which may be physically torn when the woman first engages herself in sexual intercourse. The human hymen can vary widely in thickness, shape, and flexibility. The presence of an intact membrane is often seen as physical evidence of virginity in the broader technical sense, but its absence might not indicate the opposite.

In the majority of women, the hymen is sufficiently vestigial as to pose no obstruction to the entryway of the vagina. The presence of a broken hymen may therefore indicate that the vagina has been penetrated but also that it may be broken via physical activity or the use of a tampon. Many women possess such thin, fragile hymens, easily stretched and already perforated at birth, that the hymen can be broken, or merely disappear, in childhood, without the woman's even being aware of it.

In contrast to the common cases of an absent or partial hymen, in rare cases a woman may possess an imperforate hymen, such as prevents the release of menstrual discharge. A surgical procedure known as hymenotomy which creates an opening in the hymen is sometimes required to avert deleterious health effects.

The presence of a hymen is a possible indication, but no guarantee, of virginity, given that it is speculated that some degree of sexual activity may occur without rupturing the hymen and because there may exist varying definitions as to the type and extent of sexual activity that is required to terminate the state of "virginity". This is further complicated by the availability of hymnography surgical procedures to repair or replace the hymen.

In some cultures, women are not regarded as virgins after a sexual assault, but some people disavow this notion. There are also those who take this "spiritual" concept of virginity to its maximum, considering "born again virgins" to be virgins, regardless of their past sexual conduct. However, the word "chastity" is often used in this context rather than "virginity".

In males, there is no physically visible indicator of virginity.

The status of virginity is respected and valued in certain societies, particularly when there are religious views regarding sexual conduct before marriage. A woman who is a virgin is also sometimes referred to as a 'maiden'.

Female virginity is closely interwoven with personal or even family honor in many cultures. Traditionally in some cultures there has been a widespread belief that the loss of virginity before marriage is a matter of deep shame. In some cultures (for example the Bantu of South Africa), virginity testing (infibulations) is commonplace. This would typically involve personal inspection by a female elder.

In Western marriage ceremonies, brides traditionally wear veils and white wedding dresses, which are inaccurately believed by many people to be symbols of virginity. In fact, wearing white is a comparatively recent custom among Western brides, who previously wore whatever colors they wished or simply their "best dress". Wearing white became a matter first of trendy fashion and then of custom and tradition only over the course of the 19th century.

Technical Virginity

Some historians and anthropologists note that many societies that place a high value on virginity before marriage, such as the United States before the sexual revolution, actually have a large amount of pre-marital sexual activity that does not involve vaginal penetration: e.g., oral sex, anal sex and mutual masturbation. Some refer to this as "technical" virginity.

Certain developments are bringing out the hard realities of Indian society. In an ambience of new forms of media, and sweeping societal and lifestyle changes, the psychological distance between childhood and adulthood is shrinking in the country. Many youngsters are indulging in experiments playing out adult fantasies in grown-up ways. Many young girls are queuing up before clandestine medical clinics for

Hymenoplasty, the surgical procedure that restores their hymen for future husbands. The trend for the restoration of a woman's technical virginity started decades ago in Mumbai and is fast catching up in other parts of India.

Loss of virginity

The act of losing one's virginity, that is, of a first sexual experience, is commonly considered within Western culture to be an important life event and a rite of passage. It is highlighted by many mainstream Western movies (particularly films aimed at a teenaged audience). The loss of virginity can be viewed as a milestone to be proud of or as a failure to be ashamed of, depending on cultural perceptions. Historically, these perceptions were heavily influenced by perceived gender roles, such that for a male the association was more often with pride and for a female the association was more often with shame.

The partner during the loss of virginity is sometimes colloquially said to "take" the virginity of the virgin partner. In some places, this colloquialism is only used when the partner is not a virgin, but in other places, the virginity of the partner does not matter. The archaic term "deflower" is sometimes used in modern times to also describe the act of the virgin's partner, and the clinical term "defloration" is another way to describe the event.

One slang term used for virginity is *"cherry"* (often, this is the term to refer to the hymen, but can refer to virginity in males or females) and for a virgin, deflowering is to "pop their cherry", a reference to destruction of the hymen during first intercourse.

A curious term often seen in English translations of the works of the Marquis de Sade is "to depucelate". This word is apparently a literal translation of "dépuceler", a French verb derived from "pucelle" which means "virgin" and is the root of the modern slang term "pussy". (Joan of Arc was commonly called "la Pucelle" by her admirers, most likely in reference to the Virgin Mary, another highly respected woman at that time.)

In some countries until the late 20th century, if a man did not marry a woman whose virginity he took, the woman was allowed to sue the man for money, in some languages named "wreath money".

Loss of virginity can be fatal in some Islamic countries. The custom of honor killing, which is encouraged by local custom but not the Qur'an, requires a man to kill a daughter or sister who has "dishonored the family" by losing her virginity before marriage, even by rape.

Virginity and some Religions

Virginity has been often considered to be a virtue denoting purity and physical self-restraint and is an important characteristic of some mythical figures such as the Greek goddesses Athena, Artemis, and Hestia. The Vestal Virgins were strictly celibate priestesses of Vesta. The Maiden or Virgin is one of the three persons of the Triple Goddess in many Neopagan traditions. The constellation Virgo represents a wide selection of sacred virgins.

Hinduism

In predominantly Hindu societies in Nepal and India, any form of pre-marital sexual intercourse is frowned upon immensely and is considered an act designed to bring great dishonour and disrespect to the family. "Living-in" is also frowned upon and people in a live-in relationship tend to be ostracised on all social occasions.

It is for this reason that although there is a growing tendency for Indian youth to date and choose their own partners, rather than having arranged marriages; only a small percentage of these couples engage in sexual intercourse before their wedding. This applies even to couples who choose to share a place of residence.

Due to the widespread acceptance of Hinduism in Nepal and India, arranged marriages (arranged by the parents by their choice or after comparing horoscopes) are extremely common place across all strata of society. In such an arranged marriage between a boy and a girl, who have never been married before, they are both implicitly assumed to be virgins.

On account of this implicit requirement for virginity, divorces, remarriages, widow remarriages and other relationships where the female partner's virginity is questionable, are frowned on and are hence not easily accepted by most Indians, although this is changing in the face of rapid globalisation and liberalisation.

However in cities like Kathmandu and Pokhara, the number of people losing virginity before their marriage is increasing. Due to the influence of Western movies and shows, school and college students in Kathmandu have developed a feeling that remaining virgin is not cool. This has attacked the old traditional conventions of Hinduism badly.

A study by the largest Church in Mizoram, India reveals that the incidence of pre-marital sex is high among the Mizo (natives to north-eastern India, Mizoram) youths, with 43.27 percent admitting that they had sex before marriage. As many as 52.88 per cent of the respondents said that they did not have pre-marital sex, 43.27 percent admitted to doing so and the rest refused to respond to a questionnaire sent by the Synod Social Front (SSF), a social organisation of the Mizoram Presbyterian Church. The SSF gave questionnaires to 31,202 persons across the state, of whom 30,001 responded.

Christianity

Medieval Christian society regarded the loss of virginity outside of marriage as sinful.

Until recently, some Christian states have or have had laws protecting virginity. Germany abandoned a law (1300 BGB) only in 1998 that entitled the deflowered virgin to compensation if the relationship ended. In Mexico, there is a very old saying still used by females today: "Fulfill your promise to marry me (if we had sex), or leave me how I was (virgin)".

Some Christians today say that virginity indicates a requisite state of holiness in terms of sexuality before marriage, and most Christian denominations officially follow the belief that the New Testament of the Christian Bible forbids pre-marital sex of any form. These ideas are more openly discussed throughout the Old Testament; phrases that describe sex as the union of both man and woman in one flesh exemplify the importance of both sexes remaining abstinent until the day they find spouses.

Islam

Islam provides a very strict decree that sexual activity must occur only between married individuals. Quotes such as 'Do not even go near Adultery' (Al-Israa 17: 32), are testament to this.

Qur'an 17:32 says "And come not near to the unlawful sexual intercourse. Verily, it is a Fahishah [i.e. anything that transgresses its limits (a great sin)], and an evil way (that leads one to Hell unless Allah forgives him)." Unlawful sexual intercourse in this context refers both to adultery and pre-marital sex.

Judaism

Virginity appears in Judaism as early as the verse in Genesis, referring to Eliezer's encounter with Rebekah: 'And the damsel was very fair to look upon, a virgin, neither had any man known her' (Genesis 24:16) and is a recurring theme throughout the Bible, especially with regard to the laws governing betrothal, marriage and divorce.

However, in practice, Judaism is fairly lenient about sexual relations, and has been since its early days, fairly pragmatic about the realities of sex and sexuality. Sex in Judaism is not seen as dirty or undesirable - in fact, sex *within a marriage* is considered a 'mitzvah', or 'desirable virtue'. Jewish law contains rules related to and protecting female virgins and dealing with consensual and non-consensual pre-marital sex. The thrust of Jewish law's guidance on sex is effectively that it should not be rejected, but should be lived as a wholesome part of life.

According to Jewish teaching, sex before marriage is forbidden. However, a child born of an unmarried Jewish woman is not illegitimate, and is a full member of the Jewish people. A child born out of illegitimate relationship i.e. adultery, incest and other relation types, is considered illegitimate or bastard (a mamzer in Yiddish slang) and cannot marry into the Jewish people. However, they can marry another illegitimate person.

The more liberal denominations (Reconstructionist Judaism, Reform Judaism, and Conservative Judaism) are relatively open to pre-marital sex: while it is not encouraged, it is not ignored either, and rules governing sexuality still apply. In stricter denominations, sex before marriage can be relatively uncommon, as religious practices of modesty, marriages at a younger age, and other practices, may apply.

4
Deciding to Live Together

Opposition

In the West of the world, a man and a woman who lived together without being married were once socially shunned and persecuted and potentially prosecuted by law. In some jurisdictions, cohabitation was illegal until relatively recently. Other jurisdictions have created a Common-law marriage status when two people of the opposite sex live together for a particular period of time. Most jurisdictions no longer prosecute this choice and the choosers.

Opposition to the subject of Living-in-Together without being married, comes mainly from religious groups, but also some factions of feminists too. They strongly feel that by agreeing to live-in women are offering themselves to be exploited. Opponents of cohabitation usually argue that living together in this fashion is less stable and hence harmful. Some of the opponents argue that the total and unconditional commitment of marriage strengthens a couple's bond and makes the partners feel more secure, more relaxed, and happier than those, that have chosen cohabitation. The common statistics indicates that couples who have lived together before marriage are more likely to divorce, and that unhappiness, ill health, poverty, and domestic violence are more common in unmarried couples than in married ones.

Support

In some Western nations such as the United States and United Kingdom divorce laws and family law give more rights toward women in terms of property rights, rights to male working labour of resource provision outside of marriage, sole parental and custody rights to children. In essence, as a legal institution, marriage is an obligation from a man to a woman to support her outside of marriage by the contractual obligations of divorce. In the United States women initiate 2/3 of all divorce. As a result some men choose to avoid what they see as the unequal commitment, responsibility, risk and obligation they would be subject to in the legal contract of marriage. The Men's and Father's Rights Movement and Men's Rights Activists hold similar views and seek equality in divorce and custody law.

Supporters of 'Cohabitation' or 'Live-in Relationship' advocate, in turn, cite limited research that either disapproves the claims of divorce, unhappiness, ill health, poverty and domestic violence or indicates that the statistical differences are due to other factors than the fact of cohabitation itself.

Stuff You Need to Know

When you have been dating someone for a while and decide that you are ready to live together there are things that have to be considered. You need to carefully plan and figure out all of the details. If not, you are both setting yourselves up for disaster and lots of problems. A decision to begin a live-in relationship is one that cannot be taken lightly. It is a big decision and one that will affect every aspect of the lives of both parties.

If you have decided that you want to begin a live-in relationship with a person, you need to spend time together talking about your decision. If you are not both on the same page and both wanting to live together, the relationship will never work. You will find that you have more problems which you ever anticipated. Your relationship will begin to deteriorate and fall apart. Fighting and arguing ensues and soon you are both parting ways.

The key to a successful relationship is communication. You have to be able to talk to each other and work through things. Most often problems can be resolved simply by talking. You can also prevent problems by taking the time to communicate and understand each other. It is very simple to find out how a person feels about the relationship and the possibility of beginning a live-in relationship.

Before entering into a live in situation with another person, there are some important factors to be kept in mind. Most often people that make a decision to live together have been dating for an extended period of time. They seem to understand each other very well. They both have an understanding of what they want out of the relationship. They are committed to a long term relationship with each other. They both want to be together and become close enough to where they are ready to take that next step and move forward in their relationship.

After a decision has been made to live together, there are other factors that come into play. You need to decide which person will be moving or if both people are. This can be a tricky situation in itself. The decision is sometimes dependent on current housing situations and other factors. Perhaps one partner owns their home or has more room. There children could be also involved in the decision. If you have children, there are chances are that you do not necessarily want to uproot them and move them to a new home. This can impact your decision.

No matter what the situation is, know exactly what you want going in. Do not take a decision in haste. Take the time to process everything and consider all aspects. Think about the long term consequences of your decision. Is the person that you are considering living with someone that you can see yourself spending the rest of your life with? If not, you need to reconsider your decision and not rush to move in.

Other Important Things to Keep in Mind Before Going in For a Live-In Relationship

(1) It might seem exciting and fun but keep in mind that you are not married. There is no commitment involved. You both

are just sharing a room and space. When you both live with someone you are not married to, your level of commitment to the relationship is not at its full potential. So even if you end up marrying this person, the longer you've stayed in this uncommitted mind-set, the more likely it is to stick.

(2) Be ready to compromise. There will be adjustment problems. Your partner might do certain things that drive you crazy. And he or she will not change it just because you are there so you better get used to it.

(3) You both will be financially independent but money matters will be a sore subject. Be clear with your partner from the beginning how you want to settle this and deal with it.

(4) You might feel a lack of private space when you both start living-in because when you were used to being alone and on your own, now you have to live with someone so be prepared for everything.

(5) The only time, when living together before marriage doesn't pose a threat to your relationship, is after are engaged, have formally announced your engagement and set a wedding date. Since you've publicly committed to be with each other, forever staying together at this point will make your relation more exciting and romantic.

(6) Simply think twice before deciding to live with your partner. There is no evidence that if you decide to try a live-in relation before marriage then you will have a stronger marriage.

Some Important Issues which must be resolved before deciding to Live-in Together

Before living together, there are a number of issues that must be talked about and taken into consideration:

- Are you absolutely sure about living together and have you talked about it in depth?
- Are you both mature enough to make the decision?
- Is one of the partners going to move into the other's place or are you both going to move into a new place?

- Will you split all expenses evenly and maintain a record of the same or adopt a more lenient/flexible approach?
- Would you like to make some investments together in joint names or keep all financial matters totally separate?

Live-in relationship is very popular in these days. Many young couples are living together without marriage. A long time ago it was a strong social prohibition on live-in relationship but these days youth think as compared to marriage, the level of commitment in a live-in relationship is less. But society is framed with tradition and custom which are foundational pillars. There are so many disadvantages of live-in relationship like as:

(i) It resembles a pure form of hightech adultery and fragile.

(ii) There is no concept of Husband and Wife.

(iii) It is devoid of religion, tradition and culture. Women and children are the ultimate sufferers. There is lack of commitment.

(iv) Rights, responsibilities and obligations of parties are not defined.

(v) What will be the reasonable time when parties will be treated as husband and wife, not clear?

(vi) Live-in relationship can be dissolved at any moment. It cannot build the safe and secure society.

These are just some of the many issues you may need to consider before taking the final step.

Scott Reeves, New York, USA (excerpts from forbes.com) – "Kids change everything" - Adding children to an unmarried domestic relationship makes life richer and often more complex. If children are part of your life, they need to be part of your financial planning, too.

Unlike most graduate students living together, middle-aged couples have assets, including savings, mutual funds and retirement accounts as well as a house and a car. Like their younger counterparts, it's generally wise for middle-aged couples to keep assets separate in an unmarried relationship. But think about life insurance to help your partner, and the kids, if you die prematurely.

"If one partner is not the legal parent, the best thing to do is to draft a co-parenting agreement", says Sheryl Garrett, a certified financial planner and co-author of *Money Without Matrimony : The Unmarried Couple's Guide to Financial Security*. "Like a domestic living agreement for younger couples, it spells out duties for each partner and how things will be handled if the relationship ends".

Such an agreement can guide the domestic partnership relationship, but may not stand up in court, if the couple splits. In general, the courts determine what's best for the child when ruling on visitation.

The level of complexity kids add to an unmarried domestic relationship takes drafting an agreement out of the do-it-yourself realm that can work well for younger couples. She therefore recommends getting legal advice.

In some respects, the parenting agreement is similar to working out the details of joint home ownership. In both cases, the couple must decide who is responsible for what, how much, when and how.

The possibility of a split must be considered in both instances: Who will retain the house? If the house is sold, how are the proceeds split? Does one partner have the option to buy out the other's interest and remain in the house? How soon does one partner have to vacate the house? What about relocation expenses? What about child visitation? What about the medical bills or even custody?

Blended families - 'yours' and 'mine' - are difficult enough to manage, but adding 'our' children to an unmarried relationship requires careful planning.

Children of unmarried couples are no longer classified as "illegitimate". But a child of an unmarried couple may face difficulties later in life when seeking disability benefits, death benefits or inheritance from an estranged biological parent. The situation becomes more complicated, if an estranged father dies without a will and the child has no proof of paternity.

Without such proof, the mother has little leverage if the father decides not to support the child after a split.

Garrett therefore recommends that both parents should sign a declaration of paternity and get it notarised to avoid future problems. The statement can simply include the child's full name, date of birth, sex and place of birth. Both parents provide their full names, place of birth and address at the time of the child's birth.

Garrett says listing the father's name on the birth certificate doesn't necessarily obligate him to provide future financial support for the child. But a notarised declaration of paternity signed by both parents will ensure child support if the couple later splits. However, the declaration of paternity doesn't automatically guarantee visitation rights.

Male partners in unmarried relationships should be cautious before declaring paternity if they're not the biological father. Doing so makes the male partner liable for child support until the child turns 18, even if the relationship dissolves.

It's time to think about insurance when you're young and healthy. This is especially important for unmarried couples because they don't receive many of the legal protections as married couples do have.

Unmarried partners who don't provide for each other in the event of death leave the survivor on his or her own. Remember that, in general, only spouses are eligible to receive various survivors' benefits.

Life insurance can be the key to providing for your partner. If you die, it can replace lost income for your partner and family. Life insurance can also help offset inheritance and estate taxes.

Domestic benefits are becoming more common, but are quite far from universal. At some point, it may be simpler to get married - especially if children are involved.

5

What Leads to Live-In?

Live-in relationship may be in limelight now because of the media, but the phenomena of live-in relationships are not new. It has been brought into the sphere of discussion recently, but the fact is that most of the live-in relations remain away from public gaze. The live-in relations of film stars and other celebrities all over the world are highlighted by the media.

How many live-in relations culminate into marriage is a subject matter of survey. If live-in relationships break, so do marriages. Increasingly the people are now choosing to live-in, and experts believe that one of the main reasons could be the stigma attached to a failed marriage.

Whether the live-in relationships truly benefit the couples is a debatable issue. Even if one approaches it pragmatically, it ultimately boils down to personal choice. The option to live with someone without the label of being married, or to tread the conventional path of marriage, is now a real choice that the partners can exercise.

Experts believe that given the high rates of divorce in the country, even if a woman is financially independent, the social price she pays for the failure of her marriage, is devastating. Many families still refuse to support their daughter to make her marriage dissolves.

Another point of view can be the lack of pre-nuptial arrangements in India, which adds to a woman's insecurities towards marriage. Given the Indian scenario, live-in relationships are not treated the same as marriages, so it is easier to cut all cords without having to face serious legal or societal backlash.

Divorces on the rise

Cases involving marital discord are steadily increasing in our society. The recent amendment in the Indian Matrimonial Laws to add "irretrievable breakdown of marriage" or mutual consent to get a divorce has only added a new dimension and may lead to an increase in the number of couples parting ways as the divorce process under these laws is further simplified.

There has also been a spurt in the number of cases of couples seeking divorce on grounds of non-compatibility and husbands accusing wives of "mental cruelty". No less than 50 cases are filed every month in the district courts here. During the past six months, there has been a surge in the number of divorce cases filed under the Hindu Marriage Act. The number of cases pending in the district courts has risen from 641 in March this year to 695 in July.

In one such case, the wife had sought divorce from her husband in 2004 on charges of bigamy. However, the husband accused his wife of torturing him mentally. The couple finally parted in 2009.

Another woman was forced to enter into illicit relations with other men by her husband. When it became unbearable for her she filed for divorce, which her husband granted after much persuasion in 2007.

As a result of over simplification of the Divorce Laws, the Divorce cases filed only from March to July 2010 were 305 and out of these the cases disposed off were more than 250.

Iyle e Davis (communitypaper.com) and Robin Fields (The Olympian), USA - More and more we are seeing the impact of death and divorce on middle aged and older individuals who subsequently find another partner with whom they would like to share their life. And, moreover we are seeing these life partners deciding to not get married but to simply live together.

The U.S. Census Bureau says the number of unmarried couples living together increased 72 percent between 1990 and 2000. Host of other Census surveys suggests that seniors, though constituting only a drop in the pool of cohabitants, may have met or outpaced that growth rate.

According to the Census Bureau's Annual Current Population Survey households made up of opposite-sex senior couples rose 46 percent between 1996 and 2000, a bigger jump than that of their middle-aged counterparts.

That's a rather dramatic increase. While this group may be the most low-profile participants in the 2000 Census it also clearly outlines one of the most high-profile trends. For example, a small but growing number of Americans over age of 65 now live as cohabiting couples, almost twice as many as a decade ago, census surveys show.

For older people, living together holds both emotional and financial attractions but requires shedding moral inhibitions ingrained in youth and, at times, dealing with the squeamishness of children and longtime friends.

Demographers expect the portion of senior couples who cohabit to grow dramatically in the 2010 and 2020 Censuses. For the swing generation of 60-and-overs captured in this Census, however, living together remains a liberating, if conflict-laced, option.

Though couple's reasons for living together can be as idiosyncratic as relationships themselves, researchers link the shift to other social changes.

Higher divorce rates and longer life expectancies, especially for women, mean the population of single seniors is growing rapidly, sociologists said. For younger couples, marriage often is linked to the prospect of parenthood; older couples typically are beyond this stage in life. Though eager for love and companionship, they may be skittish about formal ties.

Researchers say older women, too, can be reluctant to re-opt for marriage if they associate it with traditional gender roles played out in earlier relationships.

As potent as the emotional issues can be, pragmatism, not romance, often governs whether those older than 60 live together instead of getting married. Cohabitation, like marriage, allows older couples to share expenses, a crucial concern to those living on fixed incomes as life spans extend. Not marrying, however, means couples do not take on the financial obligations of each other's long-term medical care or mix up their retirement benefits.

While cohabiting seniors can - and often do - expressly provide for each other in their wills, unmarried partners do not have the same claims as spouses in many states. Many couples say they have left late-in-life relationships unofficial to avert conflict between the surviving partner and relatives. "We didn't want to tie up our estates," said one senior. Another said . . . "I didn't want to create a problem with her kids worrying about me inheriting part of their estate . . . and I didn't want my kids worrying about her inheriting part of my estate and short changing them."

This living together without benefit of marriage is not just an American phenomenon. It is worldwide. Even in China are following this trend.

More elderly people in Beijing have chosen to live together without getting married. Why would they choose cohabitation rather than marriage?

Many seniors choosing cohabitation say they want to get rid of the troubles a late marriage might bring about.

Yi Mi, Vice-President of the local (Beijing) elderly people's federation explains-

"People nowadays are thinking more of their lifestyles, the elderly are no exception. To some of them, walking directly into marriage can lead to problems such as property disputes. Some children dislike a re-arrangement of the heritage due to another marriage by a parent. Elderly people themselves also decline to see family conflicts due to a late marriage."

The official says many cohabiting seniors are worried about the short amount of time they will have with their new "late-in-life" partner. This new relationship is also commonly seen as negative and disruptive by the couples' previous children and creates jealousy and arguments within the family.

Moreover, official sources say the divorce rate is high among remarried elderly couples, which, in many cases, is caused by disputes over property.

Compared with youngster's living together, the society has shown a tolerant attitude towards the elderly choosing to live together.

But some legal experts are disagree. They argue that elderly people can only have their property rights protected with a lawful marriage. Shared property by cohabiting senior couples is not legally protected.

Another problem: there are heartbroken seniors whose partners pass away. They are then not recognised by their partner's children even though they have taken good care of their new lover later in life.

Elsewhere in the world, recognising the demonstrated perils of legal marriage at a young age, people are postponing marriage, or (as has been the case in Scandinavia for decades) forgoing it altogether in favour of cohabitation in record numbers.

Millions of senior citizens choose not to marry legally for a host of valid financial and emotional reasons.

There are some downsides to living together rather than marrying, however.

Unmarried partners generally aren't covered by inheritance tax laws. In most states, when an individual dies and the partner is listed as the estate's primary beneficiary, the assets are hit by an inheritance tax because the partner isn't the legal spouse.

But there's one major benefit to remaining unmarried: You don't have to assume your partner's debt, including credit cards issued by the banks and other cards. That's not the way it works for married couples - when you tie the knot, you've married the other person's debt.

No matter how devoted you are to your partner, remember this basic point: If you're not careful, risk and liability will overwhelm the love.

Many cohabiters are more like married couples than different from them - they eat dinner together every night, enjoy the company of their pets, in many cases parent children together, pay the bills, and put out the recycling. Given how often people add "Mrs." to unmarried women's names and refer to their partners as "your husband" or "your wife," apparently most people can't tell those relationships apart from marriages.

Cohabitation is replacing 'Dating'

Living together out of wedlock, once considered "shacking up" or "living in sin", has lost its stigma as cohabitation has become a mainstream.

A large difference is made within few decades. More than two-thirds of married couples in the USA now say they lived together before marriage. And the number of unmarried, opposite-sex households overall is rising dramatically.

The rapid growth of cohabitation is reshaping the landscape of family and social life in the USA.

Testing the marital waters by living together is a common practice among today's marriage-wary twenty-and thirty something's.

The number of unmarried couples living together increased tenfold from 1960 to 2000, the U.S. Census says; about 10 million people are living with a partner of the opposite sex. That's about 8 percent of U.S. coupled households. Data show that most unmarried partners who live together are 25 to 34.

"In some sense, cohabitation is replacing dating," says Pamela Smock, an associate professor of sociology at the University of Michigan. She's among researchers who are bringing attention to a living arrangement that is almost a foregone conclusion for many singles.

What's more evident, she suggests, is a probable increase in "serial cohabitation", or living with one partner for a time, then another. High housing costs and tight budgets often lead young couples to cohabit because it "makes sense to young people if they're serious about each other at all".

The logic is fairly easy to understand. "We were paying rent in two places and living in one," one says. "It seemed financially reasonable, and we're pretty compatible."

Cohabitation research published in the journal Population Studies in 2000 found that within five years of a live-in relationship, about half of couples married, about 40 percent split up and the rest continued to live together.

Reasons Older Couples are Saying No to Marriage

The U.S. Census Bureau has reported that from 1990 to 1999, the percentage of unmarried couples 65 and older rose significantly. These are couples who at one time believed in marriage. These are couples who are facing the disapproval of their children and religious faith.

It is expected that this percentage rate will continue to rise. So why are they cohabiting? For many senior citizens, marriage simply isn't financially practical.

Here are some of the reasons older couples are choosing living together rather than marriage:

(1) Tax disincentives.

(2) Loss of military and pension benefits.

(3) Fear of incurring liability for partner's medical expenses.

(4) Credit rating protection.

(5) Separation of current debt.

(6) Ability to share expenses.

(7) Health insurance.

(8) Social Security benefits.

(9) Asset protection.

(10) Alimony.

(11) The Social Security issue, however, appears to have some options:

"In general, you cannot receive survivor's benefits if you remarry before the age of 60 unless the latter marriage ends, whether by death, divorce, or annulment. If you remarry after age 60 (50 if disabled), you can still collect benefits on your former spouse's record. When you reach age 62 or older, you may get retirement benefits on the record of your new spouse if they are higher." (Source: U.S. Social Security Administration)

Step-Families

It is important to remember that a step-family, however good it might be, can never be the same as the original family. For example, one of the parents will not be the natural parent of one or more of the children. Step-families have more complicated sets of relationships to manage. There are likely to be grandparents, uncles, cousins and siblings and a parent living outside the family with no links with other members of the step-family.

You need to face a number of practical issues when you re-marry or enter into another relationship, and form a step-family. Whether the previous relationship ended through death, separation or divorce, all members need to adjust to your new relationship.

Personal Reasons Seniors are Cohabiting

(1) Anti-marriage attitude from previous unhappy marital experience.

(2) Lack of concern about what others think.

(3) Love and friendship.

(4) Children's inheritance concerns.

As a practical matter, more and more people, young and old, say living together is a requirement before saying "I do".

"I don't know how people got married before living together first", they say. *"This is crucial to see how you get along"*.

Meanwhile, societal pressures to marry before having children have decreased.

In 2003, nearly 35 percent of all births were to unmarried women, according to the National Center for Health Statistics, U.S.A. That's up from 11 percent in 1970, though the rate of increase has slowed since 1995, when 32 percent of births were out-of-wedlock. Births to unmarried teens have declined since the mid-1990s.

The stigma of having a child born out of wedlock is also diminishing and reducing.

6
Living Together - Is Live-In Relationship 'IN'

Michael Douglas, United States of America - There has been a lot of buzz about 'Live-in Relationships' these days, thanks to the recent movies but, there are still many questions about it which are left unasked. Are people actually living-in? What about the societal and parental pressures? What if it doesn't work out? Here is what the study and survey brings out:-

Couples Speak

Finding out about your partner, before making the final commitment, is often the reason behind this relationship. As call center executive Mary Johnson, who is in a live-in relationship for the past six months, remarks, "I have very erratic working hours so I want to check out if my boyfriend can adjust with me or not." On the other hand, Delhi University student Anita Larson says, "I am very finicky about cleanliness and other daily chores, so I have to be very sure about the guy I marry. I don't want these things to create problems in my life." Political Science student Ina Bliss and management student Glenn Dicks have taken an apartment together in New York City. "Right now, neither of us is ready for marriage. But, we are so much in love with each other, that we thought why shouldn't we live together?" justifies Glenn.

Among the professionals, the Multi National Company's (MNC) work culture with long working hours provides the rationale for couples opting for living together. Shruti, who works in a call centre, feels that she is open to both live-in and marriage and that her parents have no objection to it. "But, in case I go for a live-in, I would definitely want it to materialise into marriage someday", says Shruti. Management student Marry Rieger feels that it is always better to test the compatibility levels before you enter marriage. "Society attaches so many stigmas to the divorced, plus it is a messy thing to happen. With live-in relationships it can always be avoided," she says.

"I think everybody should have the right to choose who tolive with; and we talk about all the fundamental rights in this country. I think the every base of such rights should be this - the right to live with your partner," said Madhu K., a financial analyst from the city. He adds: "I think, this was overdue, and India had to wait for a long time for the court's order." Sodhi Raj, a techie, echoed his voice. "It's not a question of somebody liking it or not, but it's about one's freedom to choose who to live with. The world is getting global, and people follow a very cosmopolitan life today, we obviously can't stick to what people from the pre-colonial period have been following in this country".

Aayush Malhotra and Sakshi Kapoor's love story smacks of a Bollywood romance, starting with a ragging session in college where Malhotra was a senior student and Kapoor at the receiving end. But it was all in fun and both grew closer during their term in college and the relationship continued long after they bagged their degrees.

Their careers brought them both to Gurgaon where they decided to live in. Malhotra owned an apartment in Gurgaon so Kapoor just had to move in - that spared them the ordeal of house-hunting. They were also lucky they had their way with their respective families. As for legal acceptance - that never really bothered them. "Living together is about individual choice and not legal acceptability, they say. It's compatibility that counts," says Malhotra, who runs a construction business.

With call centre executive Kapoor's erratic working hours playing spoilsport, they get to catch up only on weekends. "Except for living together, our lives haven't changed much. Both of us spend long hours at work, eat out lot, and are penniless by the end of the month," laughs Malhotra.

The couple is, however, non-committal about marriage: "It's too early to think about and we haven't discussed it yet." But yes, they aren't entirely oblivious to the attitude society - it does put them off. "The notion that the couples have a lot of fun and it's all about sex. One should understand that it's a mutual decision, which taken by two adults despite society's rigid, moralistic stand. We took the step aware of the consequences," says Malhotra.

For many like Kapoor and Malhotra, living together is a convenient arrangement. Childhood friends Sumit Srivastava, a software engineer, and Smita Pandey, media professional, decided to stay together after both them moved to Delhi for work. Both had different working hours and saw very little each other. "It was as good as living in different cities so we decided to live in to spend quality time together. It was a well thought-out decision. We didn't rush into it," says Pandey.

Now four years into it, Pandey feels life has changed for the better. "In a romantic relationship, you never fully understand your partner. I have seen friends parting ways after a love marriage. And other side in a live-in relationship, one gets to know the partner's merits and demerits. The pressure is less compared to that in a marriage and if it doesn't work, one is free to move out," says Pandey, who feels that cohabitation makes couple more responsible. Weekends, for instance, are for finishing household work.

Cleaning up, cooking, doing the laundry, everything is a joint effort. Sumit has become more responsible. "I never thought he would change so drastically," laughs Pandey. She feels that legal cover would certainly bring more social acceptability to such relationships in the long run. "If anything, it will make house hunting smoother... but it's high time society woke up to such trends," says Pandey. Getting a house on rent was a nightmare for Pandey and Srivastava. "People treat you like an anti-social and we attract half-smiles and smirks from people," says Srivastava.

Being Indian Institute of Technology (IIT) alumnus and drawing handsome salaries weren't enough for Nisha Menon and Amit Kapoor to get a house on rent. After a whirlwind affair as students at IIT, Menon shifted to Delhi from Pune to join Kapoor as distance was taking a toll on their relationship. "We had lied that we were married. Our first landlord demanded a marriage certificate and bought some time from him citing technical reasons," says Kapoor. Menon, a consultant with an MNC has been staying with Kapoor, creative head of a production company, for the last two years. The couple says that they will tie the knot soon, but Menon avers that a live-in relationship is the best test to gauge compatibility.

The couple also had to put up with some tricky situations when Menon's parents landed in Delhi to visit their daughter.

"Every time her parents visited, I would have to pack my bags and sleep in my office. Recently, at my cousin's wedding, all my relatives wanted to know where I lived. It was tough avoiding their questions," laughs Kapoor.

Marilyn Gardner (excerpts from csmonitor) - The number of unmarried couples is on the rise, but few realise the financial pitfalls if the relationship doesn't endure. Everything looked promising for Lauren Laughead and her boyfriend when they moved from Boston to Dallas in 2002 for his job. They had been living together for nearly four years and were planning to marry. They even bought a town house in Dallas.

But their dreams were derailed two years later when her boyfriend ended the relationship. "Since the property was in his name, and he was at fault for the breakup, I just moved out," says Ms. Laughead, who handles advertising for a law firm. "I paid off my part of the credit card and left it at that. I had helped pay part of the mortgage for a year. I lost that money. He's got equity."

More than 40 percent of American women under the age of 45 have lived unmarried with a male partner at some point, according to the United States Census Bureau. In 2000, 9.7 million Americans were cohabiting with an unmarried partner of the opposite sex, while 1.2 million lived with a same-sex partner.

Unlike divorce, cohabitation offers no economic protection for either party. For married couples, there are precedents, formulas, and divorce court, says Debra Neiman, a certified financial planner in Watertown, Mass. "For unmarried folks, there is no such playing field. It's up to the couple at the onset, or early in the relationship, to set the stage and make preparations for what would happen in the event of dissolution."

Yet starry-eyed young lovers don't like to think of that possibility. "It's amazing how many of my friends in their early to late 20s go through this," says Laughead, referring to her breakup. "A lot of us go into a live-in relationship with a positive outlook. We think, Oh! Nothing bad will happen. The girl typically thinks, this is going to be great, we're eventually going to get married."

Among Laughead's friends, the woman is typically the one who moves out. She must find a place to live and buy furniture. "You realise, Oh, my college furniture - I sold that," Laughead says. "Or you have a couch and a headboard and no mattress. Those are expenses you don't think of."

Her ex-boyfriend incurred expenses, too. "When I moved out, all the kitchenware was mine," she says. "He came home and didn't have any kitchen supplies anymore."

But because her boyfriend paid the bulk of the down payment, the town house was in his name. "We figured when we got married, we'd change it to include me," she says. He was also the primary account holder on the utilities. After she left and needed her own telephone and utilities, she had no record of having a good credit standing.

Pepper Schwartz, a sociologist and relationship expert for a match making company, advises couples who are thinking about living together to ask serious questions: What are we doing here? Is this an open-ended situation that may not turn into anything? If we love each other, will we marry?

"Just because you don't like the answer doesn't mean you don't need to know the answer," she says.

In the event of a breakup, Ms. Schwartz adds, "couples must consider another key question: What do we owe each other under these circumstances - money, furniture, dogs?"

Dogs were part of the negotiations when Stacy Katz's first live-in relationship ended. She and her boyfriend had two dogs, and they were a big issue in dividing their property. Each took one.

Since then, Katz, of New York, now a manager for a financial regulatory service has had two other cohabiting relationships, each lasting about a year. When the first and third ended, she incurred no serious financial losses.

But with her second boyfriend, she learned a hard lesson after she allowed him to use her credit card. "I was the cardholder, but he had his name on it, too. When I moved away, he ran it up and didn't pay it," she says.

Katz had also cosigned a car loan. After she left, her ex-boyfriend let the insurance run out. He had an accident and couldn't pay for the repairs. "Creditors were pursuing me for a long time for the credit card and car loan," she says. That hurt her credit rating.

Laughead offers her own cautionary note to unmarried couples. "If you're paying toward something, you need to make sure that your name is on it somewhere. If the worst-case scenario happens, you want to protect all your assets."

Legal Speak

Lawyers attribute the increase in live-in relationships among the young couples to lack of patience and the inability to adjust to each other. "Everybody has a pre-conceived notion about marriage and now-a-days the couple wants to walk out of it if it doesn't work out the way they had imagined. Due to the financial independence of both partners, none of them are willing to compromise," says Leslie.

"Inability to be accountable for something reflects the immaturity of the couple these days. Earlier, in our parents' generation, the couples put up with each other. Today, the tolerance levels have gone down," adds Donna Johnson.

Approved or Not

In most cases, the parents of the couples are not told about it. That is because, though such relations are acceptable to the youth, it is still far from being accepted among the older generation, which continues to believe in the institution of marriage. Remarks marketing executive Donald Saunders, "My parents have no clue about this relationship because they will never accept it. I will tell them about us only when I am ready to marry my girlfriend."

The morality question about such arrangements brings about varied views. According to management student Jim Peterson, "If it is just to rebel against the traditional norms, it is useless and if it is to test a relationship, I don't think it is an appropriate way to do so." Rajkotia, however, refrains from labelling it as either good or bad. "It's just an integral part of the new generation where the young want to make their own rules and defy traditional norms".

It might seem exciting and fun but keep in mind that if you are not married, there is no commitment involved. You both are just sharing a room and space. When you both live with someone you are not married to, your level of commitment to the relationship is not at its full potential....

Preparing Yourself to Live Together

As the live-in relationships between adult couples cannot be treated as an offence now, the de-criminalisation might have just brought back your live-in plans from the backburner but before you jump right in, here are seven judgements which you must make in your mind.

(1) Know thy habits

If you've been living with your family or even by your own in the city, you would've already made a cocoon where you are yourself. Problem is, your love interest might just be a little intolerant towards certain bits of that. Such as taking leisurely baths; not having to wash your innerwear and socks and not sleeping before the wee hours. It's easy to say 'we'll adjust', but remember, the roots of most lengthy separation issues lie in toilet-seat habits. Guys, especially, revise your hygiene. She might not walk out on you over that but will make your mornings crankier.

(2) Choose whom to tell

We don't want to tell you 'move in when you are ready for it'. But have you considered if your core social circle is ready too? Starting off with family, in spite of live-in relationships being a reality since decades now, your folks might still think you're indulging in a blasphemous act. Tell them why you're taking this step and not only to your chosen dear one but to all who deserve to know.

Close friends would be happy after hearing this but some touchy ones might begin looking at you differently, especially those who live in denial about your relationship. Handle with care. And no need to shout from the rooftops (announcing it on Facebook or Twitter) is definitely not preferable, unless you crave attention. Lastly, that ever-curious neighbourhood aunty certainly does not need to know. Tell her you're engaged, vegetarian and religious to truncate all further questions.

(3) Love and sex will change

After all, once you begin living together, your happiness and troubles would be wed locked. A common problem is to keep your love fresh. Because you're no longer 'dating', it's crucial you constantly up the fun factor. Sometimes, love itself could be annoying: women are always known for pick up leftover bits from a meal while he switches on the TV.

For sex, however, there's good news. A live-in affair would not only enlighten you more about his/her sexual habits but your own talents and vulnerabilities. Play safe and use sex toys discreetly.

Explore your sexuality from each partner's perspective, and look at how you each engage in love, lust and sensuality in every aspect of your lives. Discover (if you can) how each planet, sign, house and aspect in your charts carries a uniquely sexual message about your inner passions, and how to give it fuller sensual expression. Do all without turning your face from social and moral responsibility.

(4) Stock up on healthy bites

Attention, all you 'molly-coddled' boys and girls. Living with your partner means living without your mother feeding you your routine cereal or your mindless midnight snacks. Before you begin losing weight and colour from your face, stock up with the essentials: cookies, dairy products and fruits. There would obviously be several dinners out of white boxes from an eatery or your kitchen, so make sure you balance that out with adequate nutrition from elsewhere.

(5) Draw a friend circle

If you really can't stand the sight of her super-loud friend, talk it out with your partner that it's either her or you. Also, his colleagues - some of whom you consider slimy - will also come and plunder your private space. Be prepared for various sets of friends coming over. Host all of them well as a couple, and not just because they are your partner's important friends. Be sure to have house parties which would mingle them all and cook together and see the love soar.

(6) Redefine life. One by two

Co-habitation, someone said, is like 'turning the TV to your favourite channel and leaving it on 24x7'. And since sharing is caring, you will need to do a one-by-two on everything, from your bed, food and often clothes. Define your daily house jobs: if you're both working and stressed, devise habits and regulations such as doing the dishes alternatively and so on.

Most importantly, pre-decide your finances. If you're moving into a pad which he/she already owns, make sure you 'give at home' enough to not be taunted and crack the relationship. Consider this a rehearsal for marriage.

(7) Unhappy ending! Maybe

Live-in relationships might be an old phenomenon but for you, it's an experiment. The chances of it working naturally well or one of you sacrificing it all to make it work are 50-50. Also, there are chances that over just a couple of months, you will discover an entirely new side of your partner which was hidden or camouflaged on those several Friday night dates. If this real avatar is unsettling you, don't live in denial. Also, in case you are driven to end the relationship, give a thought to returning to your erstwhile abodes to salvage it.

7
'Live-In' Culture Enters Indian Boundaries

At last, the concept as controversial as live-in relationship has reached India from Western shores, where relationships bounce back and forth faster than a rubber ball. The Maharashtra Government had approved a proposal on October 8, 2008, where a woman in a live-in relationship for a "reasonable period" of time would get the status of a "wife". The approval came on the heels of the recommendations of the Justice Malimath Committee, which said that if a man and a woman are living together as husband and wife for a "reasonably long period" (but it is not defined what is a 'reasonably long period' - 1 month, 6 months or 1 year), the man shall be deemed to have married the woman according to customary rights of either party.

The Malimath Committee was formed by the Centre to suggest reforms in the Criminal Procedure Code. However, by this time, only Maharashtra had shown interest in protecting the rights of women in polygamous relationships by working towards implementing some recommendations, the Centre had comfortably chosen to ignore them as they are bound to raise the hackles of the moral police.

When the proposed amendment was announced, critics immediately sprung up to say that the move would encourage men and women to get into multiple relationships outside of marriage. However, one of the major reasons for this move was that numerous women were finding it very difficult to get any assistance from men who had deserted them after living with them on the promise of marriage in the future. In many cases, the women did not even know that the man they had been living with was, in fact, already married.

As per the Malimath Committee recommendations, the Maharashtra State Government, therefore, wants the Criminal Procedure Code to be amended so that the word 'wife' under Section 125 includes a woman living with a man like his wife for a "reasonably long period". This will ensure that these women are entitled to alimony.

When the amendment came through, it, for the first time, protect the interests of women who have been taken for a misuse by uncaring men. But the state has yet to clarify how long the "reasonably long period" should be. And this ambiguity many feel may give rise to bigamy.

The Malimath Committee report also says that "a woman in a second marriage is not entitled to claim maintenance as in law a second marriage during the subsistence (the state of being supported or remaining alive with a minimum of essentials) of the first marriage is not legal and valid".

"The man should not be allowed to take advantage of his own illegal acts. Law should not be insensitive to the suffering of such women." Therefore the Committee has suggested that the definition of the word 'wife' in Section 125 should be amended so as to include a woman, who was living with the man as his wife for a reasonably long period, during the subsistence of the first marriage.

While for many people living-in is a matter of personal choice, there are todays youngsters who see it as a means of rebelling against their families or society. Two people should live together only if they are in love and seriously committed to each other, not to just share a pad and save on expenses like food and travel. They also have to be strong enough to face social drama, as most people in India still do not accept such relationships.

Unfortunately, in cities like Delhi, Mumbai, Bangalore and Pune there are many young people, especially in the Call Centre Industry, who get into a live-in relationship just to neutralise their boredom. While some end up formalising their tie with a marriage certificate, for many things go sour and they just move on.

Given this reality, the Maharashtra Government's move to give women the right to seek maintenance post-desertion or separation should be welcomed.

Approval Gives Hope To Women In 'Live-In' Relationship

The Maharashtra government's proposal to amend Section 125 of the Code of Criminal Procedure to protect the interests of a woman in a live-in relationship has been hailed as a progressive step.

The amendment, which has drawn from the recommendations made in the Malimath Committee on Reforms of Criminal Justice System, 2003, would need the Center's approval to become a law. Under the amended legislation, a woman who is living with a man as in a marriage can claim maintenance if she is dumped by her partner.

As in the words of Nirmala Sawant Prabhavalkar, a lawyer and former head of the State Women's Commission, "This is a progressive decision by the government as it would not only provide security to a woman but also make men more accountable for their actions."

Section 125 of the Criminal Procedure Code provides for giving maintenance to a neglected wife, child, father or mother unable to support themselves. Though there is a provision for maintenance of an illegitimate child, a woman in a live-in relationship has no rights that a wife would enjoy. Therefore, the proposed amendment would redefine the word 'wife' to include the woman, who was living like a wife for a reasonably long period.

Though the Government has not specified what this period should be, it is suggested to be a one-year period, by the Vice-Principal of the Society for Non-Destructive Testing, Ms. Farida Lambah. Ms. Lambah has welcomed the decision by saying, "From the women's point of view since it not only gives status to a woman but ensure that a man does not go scot-free". She believes it will make men more responsible, make them think twice before getting into a live-in relationship and even curb such relationships. "The amendment will neither harm monogamy nor encourage polygamy," said Prabhavalkar.

Pitfalls of Legalising Live-In Relationship

The proposed amendment of Section 125 of Criminal Procedure Code by the State Government of Maharashtra to include women involved in live-in relationships to be eligible for alimony from their live-in partners will have far reaching consequences, which the Government seemed to have conveniently ignored.

Granting women involved in live-in relationships a right to claim alimony is a direct insult of the most sacrosanct social institution, marriage, as in India, a marriage is a solemnised vow to support each other through thick and thin taken in the presence of community elders and with their blessings, but, in contrast, a live-in relationship is initiated by the couple just as a means to stay together. But unlike marriage, the commitment factor in a live-in relationship is very low as the ties are very easy to break. There are no liabilities involved from either side.

By giving the living women the rights of a wife (rights of maintenance) can further deteriorate the condition of the already harassed husbands (who are forced to live-in due to the unhealthy and unsatisfactory married life) trapped by their wives in frivolous cases like dowry etc. for extorting millions of bucks, in which the innocent husbands end up precious years of their life, career and prime of their youth in addition to money, while wives end up earning good amount of money either in the name of settlement or alimony etc...

But giving women an extra and added advantage over men in a live-in relationship will be highly immature on their part to assume that all relationships end due to men's fault and hence they should be made to pay for the same in the form of alimony. After totally lopsided and stringent provisions under the anti-dowry provision, it seems, that it is now the turn of live-in relationships. How any person having the slightest of common sense can draft any provision on the basis of a generalised statement that all men are criminals and all women are truthfully innocent? When there is a provision to extract money legally, why will a woman not initiate a live-in relationship, break it at will and then harass the man for their whole life.

Today's women are capable of multi-tasking and are no longer living under financial slavery. Provisions allowing women to claim maintenance under the aegis of a failed relationship, either need to be scrapped altogether or at least amended to make them gender neutral (thus allowing men also to lodge complaints to redress their grievances) and include severe and stringent punishments for filing false cases.

It is quite logical that when the woman knows that she will get money only when she put allegations, she cannot be expected to sacrifice and compromise to make the relation work. It will only be the poor man who will have to keep giving in to keep the woman happy so that she does not lodge a complaint against him and the day he refuses to do so, the woman will feel 'hurt' and seek damages in the form of alimony as proposed by the Government. Such a provision can never ensure long lasting relationships. Rather than inviting women to start relationships and end them to earn tax-free money without doing any work, the govt. needs to condemn the very idea of live-in relationships and women should not get any sops so that they are discouraged to refrain from entering the wedlock.

The shadow of doubt in a biased system is permanent as the veil of darkness remains forever. When a man is aware that stringent legal provisions are present to penalise him on harassing a woman, he will not do it on a prima facie basis. And when a woman very well knows that her allegations and tears are going to get her free money, it is highly unlikely that she is going to level true and realistic allegations. And moreover, it takes two to clap. No relationship can be single handedly initiated and ended by a man. The woman is equal partner to every phase of the relation and thus should be made an equal partner in the brunt of the fallacy as well, if unfortunately the relation does not work.

'Maintenance' For A 'Live-In' Partner Or 'Legal Extortion'?

Do Indian Men Feel Cheated?

A woman in a live-in relationship should be entitled to maintenance if she is deserted by her man, the National Commission for Women (NCW) has said.

In far-reaching recommendations to the ministry of women and child development, the commission has sought a change in the definition of "wife" - as described in Section 125 of the Criminal Procedure Code, which deals with maintenance - and suggested that it include women involved in live-in relationships.

The move aims to harmonise other sections of the law with the Protection of Women from Domestic Violence Act that treats a live-in couple's relationship at par with that between a legally married husband and wife.

NCW also sought another significant amendment to Section 125, saying that said adultery should no longer be a ground for denying maintenance to a woman.

"We have found in 70 percent of divorce cases, adultery is used to discredit the woman. Not only is she thrown out of the house, but is also disgraced and denied her rights," NCW chairperson said.

Section 125 provides for maintenance of wife, children and parents, who cannot maintain themselves. Maintenance can only be claimed by a woman who is a wife, has either been divorced or has obtained divorce, or is legally separated and is not remarried.

Pointing to the need for broad-basing the definition of wife in the section, commission officials said there are many cases where the man led the woman to believe that he was unmarried or was divorced or widowed and went through the formalities required by the Hindu Marriage Act or the custom governing him.

"Long-term relationship valid to claim alimony"

The move by NCW to seek a change in the definition of "wife" is aimed at harmonising other sections of law with the Protection of Women from Domestic Violence Act that treats a live-in couple's relationship at par with that between a legally married husband and wife.

This is a great example how desperate NCW is to safeguard the adulterous women of our society.

Their one simple aim in the name of so called Women empowerment is just to extract the money from Men as much as possible without any work and enjoy the lavish lifestyle and increase the litigations as maximum as possible.

Further the NCW does not answer, why women do the adultery and demand the Money from their ex-husbands? Such type of women should have been behind the bars, where as they are moving freely in the society as the adultery is not a crime for a Woman.

Already as per law even when a woman is caught red handed in adultery case, there is no punishment for her, in spite of husband proved the same in court, maximum the judge can refuse her claim of maintenance.

From the records it is evident, most of the women, who are well educated, working and healthy to earn themselves rush to the court and want money from the husband, but do not forget to file another criminal case (like 498 A Domestic Violence Act), mentioning that their husband ill-treat them for money, but they themselves openly demanding money as a legal extortion and that is not a crime in India. Further to note, if a woman earns the money and husband due to some reason not able to earn, even if he is ill or any other condition, he is not eligible for any maintenance form the working woman (wife).

It is hereby mentioned that, presently a woman can claim maintenance form three different Laws, like section 24 Criminal Procedure Code, Section 125 and Domestic Violence (DV) act. This is totally an abuse of Indian Judiciary System, as for the same purpose, three different cases filed and this does not only lead to wastage of Judiciary Man Power, it is violation of Indian constitution, as it clearly mentioned, for the same offence a person can't be punished more than once. Then why three different maintenance cases against a husband, if at all, considering the husband has done any offence? Further on failure of non-payment of maintenance, not only the warrants are issued, but the husband is sent to jail, loses his property under execution of the same.

In this country if a husband goes to a Higher Court feeling the order of the Lower Court is against his basic rights, he will be termed as a criminal and a new case under DV act will be filed, as it is an economical abuse to a woman.

Also the live-in-relationship, is not legalised in India, but NCW wants the legal rights to be given as same as marriage, but there is nothing mentioned, what do we mean by a living-in relationship, it can be one hour, it can be one day, it can be one month or it can be 100 years also. No doubt, a lot of countries have legalised the live-in relationship, but there is clearly mentioned, that how many years both the partners have to live together, before they claim any legal rights and the legal rights are same for both the partners, but

NCW opposes the move and wants that in a live-in relationship a man should not get any right.

Recognising the 'live-in relationship' without any prescribed time frame, is nothing but promotion of 'Animal Society', which might have forgotten by the NCW.

So, Save Family Foundation (SFF) strongly opposed these one sided laws and requested the Lawmakers to act immediately to amend the Criminal Procedure Code for Section 125 as under:

1. The word Men / Women to be replaced by the word Person and husband / wife to be replaced by the word Spouse.
2. A well-educated person should earn their livelihoods by their hard work instead of extracting money from others.
3. The word "living-in-adultery" to be replaced by the word "living or lived in adultery" during the relationship of both the partners, and neither of them should be entitled for any maintenance from each other, as it is a criminal breach of trust and cheating.
4. If anyone filed the maintenance under Criminal Procedure Code, Section 125, the person should not be entitled to file or claim any other maintenance case under section 24 or DV act.
5. The maximum Limit of Monthly Maintenance to be fixed as per Common Peoples' Living Standard only, instead of Unlimited.

Let us wait and watch that how our Lawmakers react to "NCW's claims" and able to provide and maintain a civilised society of India or create a lot of Fatherless Children in India as well, by promoting adultery and undefined live-in relationship.

So, SFF and all their sibling associations urge to the Lawmakers to make the Law without any Gender bias and without any assumption the women never lie.

The Foundation feels that such types of suggestions are insult to those honest women, who do not indulge in adultery and believe in institution of marriage.

And ironically in the present Justice system and equal rights in India, for Indian men, forget about you do adultery or not it does not matter, irrespective of the allegation is true or false, not only you, but your whole family will be thrown out of your own house or can be put behind the bars under section 498 A or under DV act, thru just one line complaint, whereas for a wife, even adultery also is not a crime, rather it is a rewarding option and free money earning business for the whole life.

After continuous campaign by SFF and their associated members against the wrong proposals of NCW, the later at last got some sense of Humanity, but they have to go a long way, as protecting and providing the shelter for the legal terrorist (misuser of section 498 A, DV act, Criminal Procedure Code, Section 125) and adulterou women is not to be termed as social service in this country and if any one tries to do that, they will be exposed in public, as the same is not good for any human society.

The question was raised by SFF and their associated organisations; at last NCW accepts their mistakes and change their stand slightly.

NCW slams live-ins of convenience

Women involved in "frivolous, casual relationships of convenience" may not get any protection under the law.

The NCW has said live-in relationships should cover only those women who have been duped or forced into marriage by men whose spouses are still alive.

During a special meeting of the committee, which is looking into the Maharashtra Government's proposal to give sanctity to live-in relationships, the NCW concluded that live-in relationships should be redefined so that women in "relationships of convenience" cannot seek maintenance or any other relief under the law. The commission, at the same time, also wants the rights of the first wife to be strictly protected.

"In certain cases where the relationship is barely six months old and there is no commitment, the court can declare it null and void. Relationships of convenience should not be considered for relief," said the NCW Chairperson.

The NCW has recommended an amendment in Section 125 Criminal Procedure Code so that it can include "women living in relationships in nature of marriage". At present, Section 125 Criminal Procedure Code allows maintenance only to a legally-wedded first wife. The second wife's rights are considered only if the first wife is dead or if she is divorced. However, the NCW wants this to be revised to include a "woman living with a person in a relationship in the nature of marriage who is unable to maintain herself". Similar changes in all the relevant laws such as the Dowry Act and the Property Act to include the rights of a "live-in" partner have been sought.

"Our laws do not recognise the rights of a second wife if the first wife is alive. However, many women are duped or forced into marriage. Such women, who have gone through the formalities of marriage, whether publicly or secretly, live in society as someone's wife and as a member of his family. Hence, they should have the right to maintenance and other property rights," said the Supreme Court advocate Meenakshi Lekhi, who is a member of the NCW's special committee.

According to Ms. Lekhi, the term "live-in" gives rise to negative interpretations. "The right to live together with a man does not give a woman the right to receive maintenance."

But, still the NCW has not clarified to the Lawmakers

- Why there could not be a minimum period of 10 to 15 years be prescribed for a relationship to be called as a "Relationship in the Nature of Marriage" as per the Supreme Court of India's guidelines?
- Why the rights and responsibilities should not be Gender Equal?
- If a Woman refuses to take the responsibility of Wife or dump the Man after a long stay with him, what kind of rights Man will have legally?

Why, when Supreme Court has directed all the State Governments to formulate law for the compulsory registration of marriage and penalties for not doing so, then if every relationship will be registered, what would be the need to legalise this so called 'Live-in Relation'?

A Taste of 'Live-in' in United Arab Emirates (UAE)

Sharjah police conducts door to door hunt for unwed couples

Yasin Kakande (excerpts from thenational.ae) - Sharjah Police going door-to-door looking for couples living out of wedlock.

Officers have already arrested one couple living together in Al Qadissiya since the new campaign began on April 19, 2010. Police say they will initially target more densely populated residential areas before spreading the net to include the whole emirate.

Police are knocking on doors and demanding to see evidence that couples under the same roof are married.

Brigadier Musa Al Naqbi, the head of Sharjah Police CID, said: "We managed to find one couple, an Arab man and an Asian woman, illegally staying together. The couple also had two children. One was two years old and the other one was four".

"This campaign is continuing throughout Sharjah because women and men having children outside wedlock are not allowed in the UAE, as well as being against Islam" he said.

Couples found to be breaking the law will be referred to public prosecutors, and lawyers say they could technically face lashes under the emirate's strict Sharia.

Salah Mubark, a Dubai based lawyer who regularly handles cases in Sharjah's courts, said: "First of all, we need to know that such cases in this country are not guided by criminal laws but by Sharia Law.

"In Sharia law the punishment for a fornicator is different to one of an adulterer; a fornicator is lashed 100 lashes while an adulterer is stoned to death."

However, Mr. Mabrouk said it was more likely that the offenders would face a prison term of less than a year, followed by deportation if they were expatriates.

Brigadier al Naqbi said the couple arrested in Al Qadissiya has confessed to cohabiting out of wedlock.

One unmarried couple who live together on weekends in Sharjah said they were worried about being caught in the new campaign.

"I am afraid to go back to his house, I don't know if the police don't want lovers to meet as well", said the Philipina woman, who works as a sales assistant.

Her partner, an Egyptian Muslim, felt slightly safer because the pair is not together under one roof during the week.

"Unless some evil person tips police that she has come, their search would most likely find me alone at home," he said.

Under federal law, cohabiting couples face two possible sets of charges depending on their circumstances, according to Jouslin Khairallah, another Dubai-based lawyer whose case load often takes her to Sharjah.

"If you have a flat with a man living in one room and a woman living in another, they would immediately face an unlawful residency charge," she said.

However, if it could be proved that the couple was sharing a room, they could be charged under "crimes of honour" legislation that carries a heavier sentence of up to three years in jail.

Responses

Riz Alvi, Dubai - It's a common practice in the world, two people living together, why is it people making a big deal out of this? No privacy even in one's own home. House-to-house search is illegal. This action by the police to enforce religious laws kind of action is absolutely disgusting and more likely in places like Somalia or North Korean, not in an Emirate with aspirations to integrate with the democratic world! Its one thing to stop public displays of affection, but when they conduct a household raid, that's despicable... this place is getting way too whacky!

Donald Glass, Dubai - Guys any idea what is meant by live-in relationship. Agreed there may be problems arising out of such relationships but they have to be supported with necessary laws (like what is done in other countries). The idea to punish guy and girl staying together has to be rethought because it is not against nature or love to live together. Please think about humanity first then religion because humans have made religions and culture and not vice versa.

What criminal act these people have done in order to punish them? Living together is never a crime. No wonder why the rate of homosexuality is increasing in this country. What will the authorities do if they find two guys or girls staying together (homosexuality is also banned in UAE)?

We need to understand that nothing is permanent except change. So please let us try to change our mentalities in order to make this country and the world a better place to live.

Abu Sumayyah, Abu Dhabi - It's unfortunate that this kind of thing has to happen to ensure that morality is safeguarded. The country should do more to make visitors and expatriates aware of its cultural and religious laws, and should not shy away from it. If people are informed in the proper way, I'm sure the expatriates would do more to respect the culture here.

I have no problem producing the required documents to prove that I am married. The fault here is not with the Government or the police, but those who try to undermine the laws of the country because of their own deluded visions of morality that they bring from especially the West. If they can't live according to the law of the country they can leave, there are many other places to go to, or they should get married and take responsibility of parenting their children rather than just "sticking around" without commitment.

8
Views before the Final Verdict

Even before the Supreme Court of India came up with its decision on the 'HOT' issue of 'Live-in Relationship', the people from all strata were gethered with their thoughts and feelings on this 'Matter of Public Concern'. Before going in the cases 'For' and 'Against' the concept of 'Cohabitation', we must throw some light on how some people have understood and explained the concept of 'Cohabitation/Live-in relationship'.

There are some who have mixed views. But the legal opinion is as clear as it gets, "There is no exclusive law that governs live-in relationship. The only remote legal angle to it is given by the Hindu Marriage Act, which again doesn't hold substance in this case. It is not contrary to Indian Penal Code (IPC)," shares Benjamin, an actor by profession. But morally speaking, the difference comes, "There is a higher risk of emotional damage, relationship complications, danger of unwanted pregnancies, in case of live-ins," he adds.

Meghna (courtesy - theviewspaper) - "Dearly beloved we have gathered here to witness the unison of this man and woman in Holy Matrimony"...a familiar statement / dialogue (Heard it almost a 100 times in myriad Hollywood flicks and tele-series)...the bride looks beautiful and the groom generally appears happy, the setting is enchanting... But the question that prominently persists is whether our life is as enchanting as expected? Is matrimony as holy and as respected?

Marriage - a word despised by many amongst us, a word that makes some jittery and yet there are others who still believe in the sanctity of such a union and respect it. It's been a while since the concept of 'Live-in' got introduced in our society and even though the Supreme Court may have granted the relationship all legalities equivalent to that of a marriage; is our society ready to welcome it with open arms?

All parents feel their children should live comfortable lives, they provide them with best possible resources, education and then wish to see them 'get settled'; in more simple terms see them get married, have a family and live happily ever after.

The institution of marriage is a very old concept. If we were to go back in time; we would not only find matrimony but even polygamy; a practice that thankfully is no more a part of our culture. It is hard to deny a fact that in a country like ours, family plays a huge role and marriage seemingly is the stepping stone or rather the foundation of nurturing this concept. The reason why marriage has been and still is (to a certain extent) a very popular institution is because it provides an individual with companionship, security and stability in life. Marriage, as argued lends a sense of responsibility in life; even though the person may or may not be ready to take this responsibility. But the traditional arguments and beliefs have not been able to restrain the current fast paced generation from finding a convenient solution. 'Live-in', a concept initially viewed as one of the adverse affects of Westernisation has now carved a niche in some strata of the society. It is no more a mere rebellious statement made by young adults but a mature decision.

Anubha, an engineering student feels there is no harm in a live-in relationship if it is a prelude to marriage as it helps one to know the better half in a better way. While there are those who second her and reason out the benefits of a live-in relationship; space, choice and just personal responsibility; a few like Ipsha feel, "It is just a matter of perception, one can take a marriage as a live-in arrangement or have a live-in like marriage".

Though such a relationship or an arrangement has always been under the ethical radar and vigil of moral police, these days it is just a matter of saving money for many. Sharing a room with a girl/boy now-a-days doesn't necessarily mean one involving a sexual, emotional connection, but it just might be more on a platonic level that helps a working professional increase his savings.

It might offer one space, help us understand our companion more but at the end of the day, many who are not against the idea of live-in still feel marriage is their first or rather only preference. "Since the court has given it a status at par with marriage, there hardly exists any difference for me, I might as well go in for matrimony as my parents believe in that", says Pranjal. Lokesh and Harshvardhan strengthen the pro-marriage case and say, "Even though such practices are not alien to our history and our present, the fact remains, that as a society for the general middle class population, living without a customary authorisation isn't and wouldn't be acceptable for a long time to come. So marriage is a must." "Besides", they add, "Some one who opts for a live-in might get bored/satisfied and leave you for no concrete reason. However in case of marriage people at least try to work it out." An optimistic Gaurav feels otherwise, "Live-in is my preference because it is time to change and evolve, though it might seem socially incorrect, but someday a change is bound to take place."

A young woman just out of school trying to adjust in college says, "It is a very practical arrangement since pre-marital sex doesn't remain an issue with the youth today and such an arrangement doesn't tie you up like in the case of marriage."

The pros and cons of both arrangements have always been before us, it is just that we do not fear the consequences any more. For those who believe it's a cultural violation it would never gain respect and for those who are moving with the times, "It is part of life and it's ever changing face!"

Either ways the choice is yours and yours alone. Like it's said, "Nothing is right or wrong: Thinking makes it so", if you feel you can't handle the responsibility, the apparent monotonous tone of married life and you need space, freedom, you may live-in; you might not be welcome but you won't be renounced either. And the debate of which is a better deal, still continues.

Nita (excerpts from wordpress) - The proposal, to make maintenance necessary for a woman abandoned after a steady live-in relationship, has been mulled over for some time now and is more controversial. Last year women in live-in relationships were legally protected under the domestic violence act and in January 2008, the Supreme Court validated long-term live-in relationships as "marriages". I am not sure what that is supposed to mean, but I think it means that the Supreme Court is taking a moral stand as bigamy is illegal in India (except for Muslims) and there is certainly no proposal to make bigamy legal.

Since then the National Commission for Women (NCW) has "sought a change in the definition of 'wife' which deals with maintenance" and has recommended that women in live-in relationships "be entitled to maintenance if the man deserts her".

And now, in Maharashtra at least, the state cabinet has given "its green signal to protect the pecuniary interests of the other woman. *If the Centre okays this proposal, this will become law.* There is bound to be a cascading effect on other states.

There has been outrage against this proposal as it is thought to be inimical to women, although the intention is just the opposite. Some believe that it will encourage people to go in for such relationships as there will be a legal sanction. The NCW on the other hand feels that it will protect the financial interests of abandoned women.

About the protests against this new proposed law, I am not sure what the protesters are against...live-in relationships from the moral point of view or live-in relationships from the angle of financial damage caused to the legal wife. I suspect the outrage is against both, although I think it is important to make a distinction between the two.

Today more and more couples from the upper classes are choosing to live without marriage. Usually such couples are both single, working, and are financially independent. The fact that they are choosing to live without marriage usually means that they have chosen to defy society and if a relationship like this breaks up it is unlikely that the woman will be in dire straits. I do not think that an educated, financially independent woman needs financial protection in case she is ditched, although she certainly needs acceptance from society, during and after such a relationship. But if the protesters feel that the proposed law will encourage these relationships and are outraged, well, I don't have much sympathy with this point of view.

The second type of live-in relationship is when a man keeps two or more "wives". This was a common practice in ancient times but today these relationships are vanished and almost disapear have gone underground. In many such cases all the "wives" are financially dependent on the man. It is one thing for a financially independent woman to go in for a live-in relationship (whether as a second woman or first), and quite another for a financially dependent woman to do so. I feel sorry for any woman who has got into a second "marriage" or live-in relationship thinking that it could well be a permanent arrangement...but when it comes to bestowing on her financial rights, then I am not comfortable with it.

I would prefer it if the court decides these incidents of abandonment on a case-to-case basis because some women deserve maintenance, if they are thrown out after living with a man for years. There have been cases, where the courts have ruled in favour of the other woman, when it comes to maintenance and I have no discomfort with that. To make a blanket law is another matter.

There are arguments that this proposed law could be misused. Law experts have said that such a law "would enable the 'mistress' to get the status of a legally married wife in all matters, including share in property, inheritance, maintenance". This is certainly not the intention of the law and in fact it the proposed law has a good intention - to help thousands of financially dependent abandoned women.

So while this law may be "revolutionary" and attempts to get live-in relationships out of the closet, it could cause harm to the legal wife. I have not heard of any other country in the world which makes bigamy illegal but allows for maintenance of a live-in partner.

There is another criticism of this proposal that, it will encourage men to stray and will overall encourage live-in relationships as it gives a legal stamp of approval to the whole thing. Well, I think the only worry would be in those cases where men go in for a second "wife." Will the law affect a man's behavior when it comes to mistresses? Well, men have been keeping them from the beginning of time and will continue to do so, regardless of the law.

But I wonder if such a law could make a man *'think twice'* about living with a woman as his wife because now he would have to pay for her maintenence even after they break up? Just as men might hesitate to jump into marriage knowing the financial commitment involved, they might think twice before committing themselves to a long-term "live-in" relationship, if they have to support the woman (and children). So while I am against such a law, I cannot help but wonder, if such a law will *'discourage'* men from keeping mistresses or getting into long term live-in relationships? If it is so, it is certainly good for the first wife if there is one, but it is hard to decide whether indeed there will be such an effect.

James Walsh (courtesy - articlecity)—The marriage is a commitment not only to stay monogamous but to be present as a social and emotional support also. After marriage the lives of both the individuals can become entwined as one and they begun to function as a single entity or unit.

Advantages of Marriage—Marriage provides one with overall stability in life. The spouse becomes an anchor, tied to which, one performs all the other functions of life. This stability is of increasing importance in the ever-changing world of today.

Marriage also leads to creation of a family unit. This family unit in turn further propagates the social ethics as are prevalent in the society. It gives shape and composure to the social set up as a whole. Marriage is not called the first building brick of the society, without any reason.

Ever since man turned into a civilised being, marriage has been the corner stone of the society. It is an accepted norm in all religions and cultures across the world. Marriage enjoys social sanctity like no other human relationship.

Disadvantages of Marriage - A marriage can have some disadvantages also. This is especially true if either one or both the partners have a strong streak of individualism. Individualism is the bane of a happy and contended married life. It can harm the relationship to an enormous extent.

Marriage means the sharing of almost everything. It is sharing of the finances, friends and family. In fact virtually everything that is there in a human relationship is shared in a marriage. Individualism is the exact opposite of this feeling of fraternity.

Individualism is an assertion of one's own self over and above the context of the relationship. Thus and individualistic person may feel entrapped in the marriage. He or she may not feel comfortable and yearn for greater privacy.

Live-in Relationships - The live-in relationship is becoming the norm in the Western societies. They are becoming so common that it is very much possible that there are more couples, who are staying in a live-in relationship as compared to those, who have tied the knot of marriage.

A live-in relationship is becoming common in the society as it does not have the strings of commitment attached to it, as a marriage does. One may not get a readymade family but then one is also free from commitments of all kind.

Advantages of a Live-in Relationship - A live-in relationship has certain distinct advantages over a married life. As has already been stated it is a relationship which is devoid of commitment. Thus it is that one can have an association with multiple partners simultaneously.

In this kind of a relationship even the financial obligations of marriage are absent. In marriage one automatically commits his or her finances towards the betterment of both the spouses. It is an integral part of married life. This however is not the case in a live-in relationship.

Furthermore a live-in relationship does not bog down an individual to the norms of the society as a marriage will. One can continue to be away from the family and friends of the other without there being any problem on this account.

More than anything else, the biggest advantage of a live-in relationship is that it can be brought to an abrupt end. In order to dissolve a marriage, on the other hand, one has to go through lengthy, cumbersome and expensive divorce procedures.

Disadvantages of a Live-in Relationship - Nevertheless a live-in relationship has got certain disadvantages also, that are associated with it. To begin with its biggest advantage of a lack of commitment on part of either individual is also its biggest drawback.

One cannot depend on one's partner to the same extent as is possible in marriage. The shoulder is there for certain occasions of problems, but it may not be there in bad times. It lacks the depth of a married relationship.

Same is true in the context of the finances. In the event of a marriage one automatically knows that the spouse is there to fall back upon in difficult times. They may in fact be sharing their finances. However in the event of a live-in relationship, this aspect is also missing.

Vinod (courtesy - wordpress) - The Supreme Court validated long-term live-in relationships as "marriages". I am not sure what that is supposed to mean.

But from my study of UK law, it could mean that the rights of the spouses will be adjudicated with reference to statutes related to matrimonial relationships. Distilled further, it means the cohabiter gets more property rights on separation. But even this, makes sense only in the literal cohabitation.

There are other pros and cons with this method. Would you be comfortable with judges passing rulings based on their individual morality? What if the judge is very conservative and sees the woman who lived-in as 'the seducer' and rules against such a woman? Legislation would more correctly reflect field research on the state of affected women and the required tailoring of remedies. But this can happen when the legislative change is made through the academic studies done by the Law commission (Is there such a commission in India? If not, then there should be one). On the other hand, there may not be adequate research on the issue and legislation can be made poorly by parties with peculiar moral values. I'm just sharing some regular legal perspectives on whether a matter should be left to case law development or whether there should be legislation.

"Why people are greedy enough to avail rights of marriage when they don't want and are not inside the bond?"

The above question assumes an unrealistic view of live-in relationships. When couples get into a live-in relationship they are not thinking in terms of rights at all. They are going in terms of informal understandings. The issue of rights comes up only when the relationship has gone sour. This is usually the case after a few years. Within that time, the woman or man may have sold his / her house and moved in with the partner. She or he may have spent loads of money on refurbishing the house, paying off the mortgage on the common home. She / he may have even left the previous job and moved town. All this will be done with good hopes and with good expectation of a life-long relationship. When the relationship breaks down, one cannot expect the partner to walk out of it forgetting all the money spent on the common home and any other losses suffered. It only makes sense that she / he be allowed to demand her share of the land.

In UK there is a difference between the way the courts approach the calculation of the share of the cohabiter in the land and that of a wife in the land. The former is based on 'trust' principles while the latter is based on statutory regulations.

In general, there is no use criminalising or illegitimating something, if the underground version of the activity cannot be controlled. Such laws are 'feel-good' laws that can placate the society but will have no beneficial effect on it.

If the man cohabiting his wife also then a cohabiter's share on separation is calculated based on the nature of interaction that have a bearing on the properties between the partners over the years. That is what I meant by 'trust principles' - a reference to the Law of Trusts. Thus, the cohabiter's share can be anywhere from 0 to 100.

But when a wife separates, regardless of the nature of interaction between the couple related to the common property she will get some rights by statute (section 17 Matrimonial Homes Act). Her share is therefore at the very least close to a 50 percent.

About live-in quasi-bigamous relationships, I may speculate, it is difficult to see that, why the wife must be given a share of what the husband spends on the mistress out of his own money, unless she has been seriously prejudiced in her living standards by the diminution in her financial allowance or if it is her money that he has been using on his mistress. I would expect the husband to have his mistress in a separate house and also have a separate bank account for her. With such separation, there shouldn't be too much of a problem identifying the property that is to be shared with the wife and mistress respectively.

Does the law classify the time period in which a couple should live together to get compensation?

United Kingdom is considering stipulating a certain duration of time in cohabitation after which the rights extendable to a wife which can be extended to a 'cohabiter'. They're doing this in light of the fact that the number of cohabiting partnerships are on the rise and constitute a significant portion of marriage-like relationships. Many of these couples even end up raising 3-4 kids and buying and selling 2-3 homes. There remains little to distinguish them from an actual marriage. They have good social research and good deal of case law to back their laws. So far, the law commission in UK has refrained from specifying a time period. But they have put it as a recommendation to the Government. It is now up to the Government of UK to come up with legislation with this detail.

I really don't understand why people opt not to get married even when they have kids. Strange! One of the reasons that I've heard is that "marriage adds everything and nothing to the relationship". Make of it what you will.

Bottom line, marriage as a ritual loses all meaning. This is particularly true of cultures where individualism is celebrated. Individuals see themselves ungoverned by society with limited obligations to the society as a whole. They also expect little from society. The society is not seen as greater than the sum of individual actions. In fact, they only see individual people around them and not a society as an entity. Therefore, they see their actions as having little or no impact on the society.

In my mind, the only philosophical argument that remains for marriage is that of preserving the institution of marriage in society as a symbol of commitment to family values. These rituals are occasions for symbolic representations that individuals make towards the society. They are a part of it and the society in turn makes its representation to the couple by its acceptance of the relationship. In this manner, there is an addition to the 'mythos' of the society. The need for such interaction with the society as a whole is only felt where the boundary between the individual and the society is not so sharply defined. The individual actually sees an entity called a society around him/her that has a collective personality to it.

That's just the way things are. I am not being prescriptive about the correct philosophy for a culture. Erosion of individuality brings its own burden which I wouldn't want to get into in this comment section.

It is interesting to know that the UK is considering a legislation to legalise the live-in. I guess for them the reason is different, that so many people are living as without marriage. In India it is only a small proportion of people. Most of the cases are a bigamous relationship where poor women are exploited and that is whom the Government wants to protect.

In Germany indeed, after a divorce, the richer partner has to support the poorer one if in need and the children. But statistically speaking, it is still the wife who is financially dependent on the man even here, especially in couples with children. Many live-in couples here have children together and do not marry because they do not believe in it. In such cases, when they split similar laws apply like in divorce cases. If a couple splits in a live-in relationship and have no children, the woman cannot claim alimony. Only if they have children, since she / he has dropped her / his career in order to bring up the kids. In the UK, I guess there is no difference between long-term live-in relationships (de facto) and marriages. The woman is always favoured in case of divorces in the UK.

Khadija Ranjha, Pakistan (from - theviewspaper)—A walk down a flower laden aisle, circles around a sacred fire, or even simple signatures on a document; marriage has a different representation in different people's minds, but for all, I am sure, its sanctity is utmost. A very normal situation has now arisen, that is slowly replacing these images, and that is of a live-in couple.

A live-in relationship is one in which two people, who are not married decide to live together in a house or flat and share a bedroom. If this idea was presented to our grandparents, they would gape at us, open-mouthed, and demand to know what devil had possessed us and made us think such insane thoughts! And who can blame them; such a situation is a very new one in the subcontinent, and has only started becoming popular over the past few years, and in essence, is preposterous.

People have become increasingly independent, and choose to live according to their own views, wants and needs. But the fact that the idea of live-in relationships is popular does not justify that it is absolutely correct and acceptable to all. Living in a conservative society, where only two decades ago, if a man and woman who were not legally married and were not from the same family, were seen together in public, were arrested on the charges of 'Zina' (pre-marital sex and adultery); the idea of an unmarried man and an unmarried woman living together is considered highly incorrigible. And with good reason too, for I have grown up being told that marriage holds more importance than any other relationship, and such a relationship is a violation of that very thought.

Pakistan is an Islamic country, with a clear majority of the people being Muslims, and in our religion, there is a strict rule against pre-marital sex; a live-in relationship negates that very rule, as a couple that is living together is bound to be sleeping together too. In short, from a religious point of view, it is an unethical and immoral practice. Socially, live-in relationships are not that widely accepted in the sub-continent, and are a common practice only in sprawling metropolitans like Mumbai, in India, and Karachi in Pakistan. Cities like

Delhi and Lahore are, however, comparatively conservative in such matters.

The reason that such a category of a relationship took form is because of the highly promoted Western culture. Live-in relationships have been promoted by the media, even in Bollywood movies like, *Salaam Namaste,* which was actually a very bold step for the film industry. In reality, such relationships are not widely accepted and not common place, at large. Such false depictions are spreading this trend in the upcoming generation, and are actually leading to threaten the integrity of the concept of marriage and are corrupting the sanctity of it. If a couple is ready to share all aspects of each other's lives, they may as well enter into a marital union, rather than ruin the concept of it.

The generation gap between our generation and the one before us is a very wide one, so the introduction and promotion of such ideas is going to widen the gap. Insightful communication is the only option that can help - bridge that gap, but even though the previous generation is what we now call "old fashioned", their policies seemed ethical enough to work. We need to take a leaf out of their book, and incorporate their views into our lives, for some of their concepts and practices seem far better than ours, now.

Neel (from - wordpress) - "[In the future] we may have a formula for making marriage more democratic and egalitarian between men and women. But that formula will probably leave us with a less stable kind of marriage than we once had because ... [it's] based on voluntary commitment. People get to choose not only whether they marry, but whether they stay married on the basis of how satisfied they are.

So the trick is to develop marriages that are fulfilling, but at the same time have a good chance of lasting a long time. I think we might be on the verge of a new kind of relationship."

So, what is 'marriage' and what is 'live-in' anyways? Love is not hereditary... but marriage is: If your parents never had it, there are no chances you having it either! (That's the way it is in Indian culture - at least so far anyways.)

I agree that there are pros and cons in all situations. However, it's not just about taking some decisions; it's about sharing lives, sharing everything, blending into each others' families. I may be wrong, but I feel that breaking a 'live-in' relationship is a more easier than breaking a marriage. One would try harder to set things right in marriage rather than 'forget it, it won't work out' mindset in 'live-in' relationship. I do agree that a live-in relationship indeed has its own good points as well.

The argument is that the live-in relationship can be used as a pre-marital arrangement to find out the compatibility of the partners - which is a fallacy. The very essence of marriage is understanding and adjustment, which cannot be expected from the live-in relationship. **By accepting to a live-in relationship the couple agrees that they are not in favour of any adjustments and understandings.** Here I would also like to talk about love marriage and arranged marriage. **Here again it is statistically proven that love marriages are much more fragile than arranged marriages, which itself counters the argument that pre-marital relationship helps in finding compatible partners!**

But I believe that if a couple decides to have a live-in relationship instead of marriage for the convenience, it should be fine (for me it's not). In today's life some people have different meanings of life. A carefree life where personal comfort and spiraling career is more important.

According to Jim Peterson, who studied the subject of live-in relationships—**"If it is just to rebel against the traditional norms, it is useless and if it is to test a relationship, I don't think it is an appropriate way to do so. I would, however, refrain from labelling it as either good or bad. It's just an integral part of the new generation where**

the young want to make their own rules and defy traditional norms".

One more thing I don't like the idea of 'live-in relationship' is because I think one would opt for live-in relationship when you want to "test-drive" the relationship (more like buying cars, if you didn't like the test-drive you won't buy it) and hope that either it'll work out the way according to how you want or you will find a better partner and I think one can **never** be happy in life with such attitude. Everybody has to compromise a lot in any relationship and frankly speaking that's the beauty of it!

Yes, sadly I'll have to agree that there will be situations where live-in won't be worse than broken marriage (doesn't necessarily means it's better though). However, we must understand the difference. I can pretty much say that above 90 percent of those who opt of live-in don't have slightest clue of what it means! I've almost always heard people talking about it as a "test-drive". They want to see if it "works out" or not. That is insane and way far from truth. You can 'Never Ever "test-drive" a relationship. Following is what I feel:

Marriage is for you if ANY or ALL of the below holds true

(1) Basically, if your goal is to find a suitable match and if you want to know if it will work out or not BEFORE you get married then live-in IS NOT FOR YOU!!!!!!!!!!!!!! Marriage is!! (If your end-goal is to get married, even 4-5 years of "live-in" won't tell you much!! There are, were and always -will be compromises involved in a marriage!)

(2) You want to have a family, a wife and kids, and career is not the only thing in your life. (Doesn't mean career is not important)

(3) RESPONSIBILITY is the key word here.

You are cut-out to be in live-in relationship if ALL of the following holds true

(1) You NEVER EVER want to get married AND NEVER EVER want to have kids.

(2) You don't care at all about having family (or don't want family at all) the only thing you want to focus is your career.

(3) You don't want to have compromises and believe in "my way or highway" policy.

(4) 'LIABILITY' is the key word here, no responsibility!!

There are many immature people who confuse and mix live-in as a test drive of a relationship or like a preview of a movie. Don't forget, previews are always meant to be exciting!! It doesn't always tell you much about the movie. Do not have false or unrealistic expectations from "live-in" and one must not think about live-in if, in the end, you do want to get married and settle down.

Srishti Gupta (from – the viewspaper) – Live-in relationships may soon be legalised in Maharashtra, India, and this has ignited a fresh round of debate across the nation. But according to me, the idea proposed by the Maharashtra Government is logical on grounds of practicality and rationality. The Government has proposed an amendment to the Criminal Procedure Code whereby a woman living with a man 'for a reasonable amount of time' would be given the same status as a wife, the right to inheritance, maintenance as well as alimony. Well, this is definitely contentious to all those hypocrites who reign strong in the Indian society. It is to be understood here that there are sufficient number of people in urban areas opting for live-in relationships and legalising it ensures that no one involved is exploited. But it is intrinsic that the process and fashion of legalising be such, that live-in relationships serve the purpose of providing an adequate groundwork for a lifelong commitment.

Well, before I elaborate on the utopian concept, I just proposed - let us have a look that why people enter into a live-in relationship and how should the notion be legalised to reap the best results. The most basic cited reason for entering into a live-in relationship is to get more time to take a decision for a lifetime. Many people who don't want the tag of "marriage" at a certain stage in life also second the idea of cohabiting, whereby they can feel free from any kind of social and personal bindings. However, people who condemn the idea of legalising it say that it would just encourage the undecided and rash youngsters to continue play frivolously with significant issues like commitment. But my humble contention here is, if the idea is legalised with adequate constraints then it has equal chances of helping people take wiser decisions. In the first place, it will ensure that people indulge in profound brainwork before going in for cohabiting because of the legal consequences associated. Couples will also have the freedom to end the live-in relationship before a certain time if they don't find each other compatible. It will also grant live-in relationships a more serious and responsible nature.

It's very important that there should be clarity in laws about who can enter into such relationships or else it may contradict the Hindu Marriage Act which clearly screams that a person cannot have two wives simultaneously. A fixed specified eligibility criterion will help stabilise the cases wherein people who are already married enter into these relationships, which in a lot of cases causes the exploitation of previous partner's rights. Associating legal constraints may help in bringing down the soaring toll of divorces in the country too.

The present intelligentsia unanimously and aggressively demands time and leeway to choose their partners which can be given to them by legalising the concept of living together before marriage for specified time duration. All those so-called commitment phobic people who don't want to undergo a ritual called marriage certainly deserve to have a lifelong socially respected relationship. Legalising silently serves this vital purpose of giving the status of husband and wife to a couple living together for certain duration of time.

I feel that though live-in relationships might sound more like a Western concept but it isn't very tough to implement in our swiftly changing society too. But it should be legalised in a manner which is constructive for people entering into it and also benefits the society at large.

Sameera Ahmed (excerpt from youth ki awaaz)—India has long been a conservative country with conservative people having conservative thoughts.

Ironically the land of the Kamasutra (an ancient Sanskrit text giving rules for sensuous and sensual pleasure and love and marriage in accordance with Hindu law) has always had an unadventurous outlook towards the concept of marriage and relationships.

Marriage has different meanings in different people's minds. But in India, whether you individually believe in it or not, matrimony is sacrosanct. It is not just the union of two people legally; it is the union of two souls and their families. The couple gets the blessings of their elders and they live happily ever after. Relationships out of marriage are looked down upon.

But today marriage doesn't hold the same values anymore. Divorce rates were practically unheard of until a decade ago. People have found new ways to live those, which are more convenient for them. Cohabitation or the concept of a live-in relationship is one such consequence. Some people think of marriage as an obstacle; like a mountain that you are forced to climb not knowing what's at the peak.

For such people, a way out is the concept of live-in relationships. No marriage, no pressure, no strings attached. Live for the present with the person you want to be with - that's the mantra. And it sounds too good to be true.

In some of the states (such as Virginia) in the United States of America, living with your partner before marriage is illegal. People who lived like that were shunned in their society half a century ago. But at present, live-in relationships are being accepted. However, my point is, that parents blame it on the big Western influence. We say, why blame the West, when we are at fault? We have our own minds. We do something because we want to, not because the rest of the world does it. Just because our country considers such customs as immoral, it doesn't mean that people who follow it are morally loose.

Why India hates it?

On one hand, a live-in relationship could solve all the problems that a marriage would create. Usually people in a live-in relationship see themselves married together in a couple of years. Some do it to check their compatibility with their partner, some do it to avoid the legal hassles of divorce in case the relationship falls apart, and some do it because they don't believe in needing to prove the society that they are ethical in thinking. However, marriage enthusiasts say that a live-in relationship is more liable to break; destroying the chance that a marriage could have saved. Studies prove it too.

The whole question comes to India's culture. A marriage can be a bed of roses but it also means tolerance and adjustment. After marriage People do fall in love with their partner in marriage *filmi ishtyle* (as shown in Indian films) but a lot of people adjust, fight and tolerate the marriage because divorce sounds too uncomfortable to handle. Cut to a live-in relationship, and snap! If you don't like it, you are out of it.

The metro lifes are fast catching up on this new, easy to handle trend. But if it is tred this in the towns and villages; a father would rather murder his daughter than be a witness to her committing such an atrocious 'crime / sin'.

My verdict

It is against our very upbringing. But like most things, even this will also change. In 2008 four Indian cities Delhi, Bangalore, Puducherry and Kolkata held gay parades for celebrating greater tolerance and living towards the third gender. In a situation like this, can welcoming the idea of live-in relationships be far behind?

I used to believe that we, as the youth are ruining the essence of Indian culture. But after asking tons of people mostly youngsters that what they felt about live-in relationships I have a dilemma. Most said "It's a matter of personal choice. If someone wants to do it, let them. It's a free country. But I would never ever go in for it or recommend it."

I am still wondering if I should be proud of our inherent morals or flabbergasted at our conservative thinking right in the 21st century.

Is it time when we should review the social sanction granted to the institution of marriage or is live-in merely a matter of convenience? Let us see what people replied when asked if 'Live-in' relationships be legalised?

Agreed

Dr Rajlakshmi Darbari, author of the book Knowledge of Love and Healing (Marriage University) says, "Couples who go in for Live-in Relationships, are looking forward to having sex everyday without a lifelong commitment. They come together basically just to have sex and then after living together for some time or for years, then they begin to wonder what is marriage..."

Dr Rajlakshmi says especially the women, they believe that in a Live-in relationship the man should totally act like a husband and be faithful only to her. Men usually think that this arrangement is so I can have sex every day, but doesn't tie me down to just one woman, I can change her, if I find somebody better or more attractive etc. I am free to walk out whenever I want.

Thus in these relationships people start playing mind games on each other and start reading books which teaches them how to catch a man/woman and keep forever. These couples, don't understand what they are doing together and can't answer simple questions like, "Do you want to marry her?" The answer usually is I don't believe in the institution of marriage, it's just a piece of paper. Instead of answering the question, they try to justify their act by destroying the marriage institution. So where does this all lead to in the end? The answer is nowhere. So to catch the man the woman has to get pregnant to be mother of his baby.

In all these encounters we only see psychological games being played, and then pressure being put or emotional blackmail begins. The only answer then they found is we should now get married; we are going to have a baby. So where is the concept of a pure divine love marriage?

If the couple after living together for ten years gets married does that mean it's a pure divine love marriage...?

James Ritchie, London, U.K. - Three things

(1) Equality of genders: If indeed there is such a thing (Personally I do not believe in it) then there should be no provision for a man to pay for the upkeep of the woman. Between consenting adults maintenance should be paid to the person irrespective of gender to whoever who cannot afford to keep themselves. Children should be raised by both the partners. Very honestly I would not get in to a relationship where I am expected to feed everyone.

(2) Legislation on private matters: Who I sleep with, what I do in my own bed and within the confines of my own house is my own business. I do not like the whole tone of the Government here. Let's legalise this or that. Human relationships do not need Governmental sanction. It sounds very patronising to me, I do not know about you guys.

(3) Marriage/Long-term relationship: The whole point of not getting married is that you want to stay with someone without committing and being able to leave whenever you want to. It is about retaining your independence. Financial independence is a great part of that independence. If I wanted to share finances with my partner(s) I would simply marry them! This law 'legalising' long term relationships is cleverly just trying to take out that option by converting a long-term relationship in to a marriage.

Men and women enter such relationships by their own consent and as such should be responsible for their own actions. There are obviously some women who have multiple partners. It works both ways, men polygamy as well as polyandry. All I am trying to point is that making gender specific laws does not help. If in India, you must legislate, legislate for humans, not for men or women.

Marriages and domestic partnerships are regularly registered in most of the world. I see domestic partnership as an in between Marriage and just living with someone. If I am not wrong the Indian Government either is already registering all marriages or plans to do so eventually. Domestic partnerships can eventually be a solution for people of minority sexual orientation to get a sort of legal protection for their "relationships" if they want so.

Marriage is indeed a legal / social sanction of relationships. Live-in relationships should not come under purview of the law; a legal commitment to a lesser degree can be incorporated in to the law by keeping the doors open to "domestic partnership" between two consenting adults irrespective of gender. All you need is a register for such relationships. I suggest the registrar who is usually the 'Tehsildar' (a Government appointed caretaker) in most Indian districts can do that job. It's as simple as that.

Rabina Sheikh Kapoor, Kanpur, India - Legalising 'Live-in' is a good move, given the propensity for young couples to prefer live-in relationships. Legalisation not only aids in minimising the stigma associated with such couples, but also provides a level security to the people involved in the relationship. It is common for married couples seeking divorce to turn to the law for resolving monetary conflicts, because both in the relationship have had to invest in it in various forms. t is normal for guys and gals to get tired of a relationship and abandon a partner in the live-in arrangement each other with relative ease. This legalisation will not make dumping so easy!

It's time we let go out of the orthodox lifestyles of the Mughal / Victorian era's. Most people talk about the Indian culture, so, just want to remind people that the 'REAL' Indian culture is one from which the Kamasutra came out.

With huge emphasis being laid on the sanctity of the institution of marriage...I think it's not Live-in that's promoting prostitution but marriages are... A contract where incompatible couples are forced to live together for a prolonged period of time, as the society does not accept divorce so easily nor has taboos associated with it. As for abortions...does a marriage dictate that an abortion cannot be done? Let's be practical. What we have now is a 'bastardised' version with massive influence from the strict Islamic and 19th Century Christian culture. The West has moved on new progressive thought It's time when we should move on too.

Vishal Gupta, Mumbai, India - There is nothing wrong with a live-in situation. Different people see marriage differently by their own view. Some use it to lose their virginity, some to get dowry; some see it as a business deal, some to have children, and so on. Only a few marry for love. So a live-in relationship makes so much sense. There is nothing bad in it. Now in this era of modernisation, we should change our mindset.

Live-in relationships will be there even if we don't legalise. Around twenty years before we used to criticise the West for this sort of living and declared it as "against social norms". In India where a film song which starts with an abusive expression creates so many problems, but fortunately we are changing and have already changed a lot and we do the same things what the people in West did some years back. Time will always tick and so is the culture going to change. This doesn't mean we should be barbarians. But it is better not to carry the overload of fake morality.

This should be legalised immediately as one can know about the other persons' habits, his merit and demerits also. The dowry and divorce will come down. They can also know about their family attitude and discipline.

Ashish Dholakia, Surat, Gujarat - I fully endorse Cohabiting. It's a new trend. Otherwise also in married life, it is not certain that everything will go well.

The live-in relationships are not wrong but must be governed by certain strict laws. These relationships are good for divorced guys and the people, who could not get married at the right age may prefer to be in live-in relations.

The shape of society is changing as such the methods will also go for a change. Fruitfulness will depend on maturity of partners. One day it may be a natural way to live. So there is no use criticising it. I am in favour but with certain conditions and regulations as well.

George Demetriii, Trento, Italy - I do support the concept of Live-ins... They do have a lot of positive points...

We can always know your partner well before getting married. When we date someone, we always see the best of them, but when we live with someone, we can see them in their best and worst. We would always love to live-in with a person for whom we have strong emotions So live-in provides one with a good outlook of what a person is like whom they are thinking of getting married, but then on the other side live-in requires high level of maturity and responsibility. People who may get into live-in just because it's cool or without knowing what it's all about, are in for big trouble...

Marriages are important because they provide security to the people... that's why they have been happening since years and will be happening in future too...

So, live-in should not be a substitute for marriage... let it be a step before marriage... that's a balanced way I guess...

Hardik Mehta, Gurgaon, India - The question over here is the concept of live-in relationships and not the affairs. I know in affairs there are physical relationships as well as one night stands for the unmarried girls, but with live-in relationship, you are actually living as husband and wife without getting married. This is totally different since the persons involved are staying together and their parents also know about their relationship.

I am not talking about the system in UK. In UK / US, the parents encourage having the boyfriends / girlfriends and also having the night outs at one of the friends' homes. Like before purchasing the car, you take the test ride, similarly before going to the long term relationship you start knowing the person fully while staying together.

Coming back to Indian culture, the traditions and culture has to change with time. This is also told in ancient mythological books. Nothing has to be stagnant and with the passage of time, the new things should be always adopted. The flexibility should be present in the culture and laws.

Dhananjay Wagle, Osmanabad, India - The legalisation of 'live-in' relationships in Maharashtra has raised a great controversy all over India. But then the question that arises here that, why is it that more and more people prefer to have a temporary live-in than to have the permanent baggage to a marriage? How come a society as conservative and as traditional as the Indian society has given place to an idea as modern as 'live-in'?

Marriage is considered to be the sacred bond between a man and a woman. So is the concept of 'live-in' immoral? Just because there is no law in support of the concept of live-in it is looked down upon. When the Government is ready to acknowledge the existence of live-in relationship in India and is making legal arrangements, why it has become a social issue?

There are many individuals and couples, who are in support of the legalisation of live-in relationships in India today. The very famous film maker, Shyam Benegal told Press Trust of India (PTI): "It a very good step as it will not only protect the rights of women who enter into a live-in relationship, but will also be helpful to the children from such relations in getting their rights in future." A very valid point indeed, but besides the issue of security it is also a matter of personal choice.

The truth is that a live-in relationship is a healthy way of avoiding the baggage which comes with a marriage comes. If two individuals are willing to experiment with their relationship, then what right does the society have to interfere in the personal life of two individuals anyway? And honestly, the society comes in the picture only during the whole ceremony of marriage, 'to grace the occasion with their presence'. But when a couple is getting divorced, it's only the two that stand before the court of law. Then why is the so called "concerned" society raising its voice against the live-in relationship?

It is only the age old tradition that they are trying to save. Then why do only that in the marriage department? If India is going all global and tech savvy and opening its arms to everything that comes with a tag with "international quality", then why don't we just drop the hypocrisy and accept live-in relationship as the reality of the day. It's after all happening all over the world. Making it legal is only an obligation. And practically speaking, how exactly does it matter that anything is legalised in India?

Aarlin, Bangalore, India - In my opinion everybody has right in India to live according to his / her own methods. So if a couple have understanding and ready to live together, then what is the harm in it. As India is known for its cultural diversity, one culture can be live-in relationship. It is very rightly said, "If You Follow All The Rules, You Miss All The Fun".

So, it is fun to have live-in relationship. After getting bored from long office work an opposite sex person can give some better relaxation.

Denis Lindey, Cambridge, U.K. - Ever heard of try before you buy?

I think it's a good idea to live together 'BEFORE' you get married to see how compatible you are for each other. It's easy to hide certain 'annoying' habits when you only see each other the odd hour here and there.

I think marriages have lost their appeal to the younger generation, because it means commitment and not many people can handle that (along with faithfulness). Younger generations feels marriages involve more legal problems and are sometimes considered an unnecessary, time consuming and expensive ritual. However it depends on your religion and your beliefs.

Shikha Sukur, Satara, Maharashtra - I am in fact a supporter of the concept live-in relationships in India. Though, there are many points against the concept of co-habiting which can be put forward as follows:-

1. Live-in relationships are against the Indian culture. A man and woman cannot live under the same roof, if they are not married.
2. Live-ins are more like an 'experiment'. If it does not work out, what will the society think of the woman who had sex (assumed in this kind of relationship) with a person who was not her husband?
3. The orthodox mentality of parents. You would be hurting them if you live-in.
4. What happens if you are in a live-in and your partner decides to leave the city? Would you support his / her career?

Irrespective of the above said short sighted, so-called problems with live-in relationships, in my view it should be made legal. In today's modern world relationships have changed drastically from the "primitive ghetto society" (an ancient Yehudi culture). Now each person must have one's personal space. Instead of lifelong commitment in marriage it is better to have agreement on live-in. If both partners get attached, later they have an option to marry. In fact personal sphere should not contradict with family sphere. In that way one can still give commitment to family. So live in should be permitted as part of one's private personal life.

A very large number of married couples are unhappy today. The partners have to seek emotional and physical support outside of marriage. This has caused much tension in the society and has lead to violence. A private legal live-in relationship will ease these tensions.

Zeeshan Ameen, Hyderabad, India - I have always been pro legalisation of live-in relationship, by legalisation I do not think considering it as a marriage makes sense. I think there is a blurred line in my mind when I try to differentiate between a legal spouse and a live-in partner. One very interesting thing is that this could well be on the lines of legalising bigamy. It would be interesting to find out the laws in other countries regarding this. May be with all these legal changes, the concept of live-in might dwindle a bit.

As a common man, what amuses me is the social protocol, should one really worry so much before deciding you want to stay with someone? I do agree that there are some social and moral responsibilities, more than all this I would say both the individuals have personal and human responsibilities towards each other, if they don't I am sure they would never agree to live-in at the first place.

Pachaimuthu, Nallur, Tamil Nadu – Before criticising the issue of legalising live-in relationships, we must first understand that why it is required? We should see the other side of this law helping women, who get cheated by men by hiding the fact that he is already married. In such cases, if a woman complains of fraud, we should have a clause in law as to take out double money from that man. After all, he cheated and deserves no love, commitment and sympathy.

Fateen, Orlando - So what if two people don't want to get married? If they are living together long enough, why they should not get the benefits? I think extending the benefits of marriage to live-ins is a good thing. It's not just about maintenance. Even things like insurance, for e.g., a live-in partner can nominate the other person. And I don't think live-in partners necessarily keep finances separate. So long as it doesn't harm others, I think they are fully entitled to such benefits, for which we need to go back and think about why the concept of maintenance emerged, in the first place. It is more important to do with traditional division of labour, than whether a relationship is a marriage or a live-in.

However, I don't think we should confuse live-ins between single people, with bigamy, which is a live-in where one person is married, and the other isn't.

Dhanraaj, Basildon, Essex, U.K. - I am very much in favour of live-in relationship as the kind of flexibility it provides. So it should be legalised as early as possible. But some questions linger on in my mind:

1. Will this law apply to gay relationships too?
2. Can a married man or a married woman have another gay or lesbian relationship respectively?

So guys, I hope you can see how utterly illogical the laws can be....

This is such a waste of time and money, according to me... Why bother with trivialities? If people want to live together, they'll do so and there is no harm in it as far as they are satisfied in this kind of relationship. I know friends who've been living together for more than three years... It's just one insane law after the other, it seems...

Disagreed

Cohabiting couples should not be given the same legal rights as married people, an influential think-tank will say today. The **Centre for Social Justice (CSJ), United Kingdom (UK),** set up by former Tory leader Iain Duncan Smith claims the change proposed by the Law Commission would 'fuel family breakdown'. The CSJ wants a shake-up of the law to strengthen marriage as per their July, 2009 proposal.

The group argues that this would combat social problems, as children of families that split up are more likely to do worse at school, suffer poorer health, fall into crime or drug abuse and be unemployed.

Fathers will also get new rights to see their children after a divorce and grandparents will be allowed to remain in contact with their grandchildren if their parents split up.

Mr. Duncan Smith said the report was 'timely' because of public concern over the case of Baby P, the 17-month-old toddler left to die in a bloodstained cot after suffering unimaginable brutality at the hands of his mother and her live-in boyfriend.

He said the case shone the spotlight on the chaotic nature of family life in the poorest parts of Britain and proved the urgent need to shore up traditional relationships.

"This review is working from an underlying assumption that marriage should be supported both in government and in the law and that, related to this, fatherlessness - or motherlessness - should be avoided," he said.

'Policy can and should be focused on stemming the tide of relationship breakdown. Marriage acts as a stabiliser and a signal. Married couples are far less likely to break up than couples who live together without getting married.'

The Centre for Social Justice (CSJ) - whose ideas have influenced Conservative leader David Cameron's family policies - was publishing a raft of proposals in its report The Family Law Review.

They include making pre-nuptial agreements - popular in the United States among celebrities and the super-rich - legally binding. The contracts set out exactly how money and property is shared out if a couple ends their relationship.

Under the current laws - opposed by senior members of the judiciary - judges can only take 'pre-nuptials' into account during divorce proceedings, and can't be tied by them. But the legally questionable status of pre-marriage agreements deters couples, especially the wealthy, from walking down the aisle.

Experts say it would also spell an end to costly legal battles such as the £10 million divorce of Sir Paul McCartney and Heather Mills if England and Wales were brought into line with other countries.

A string of Family Relationship Centers would also be established to prevent divorces ending in acrimony, which could damage children.

The CSJ also rejected proposals to give cohabiting couples the same legal rights as married people, is warning to this would 'fuel family breakdown'.

The Law Commission wants people to be allowed to claim financial support from partners, if they had lived together for a set period of time, a so-called common law relationship.

But the report said: 'While doing much to address perceived injustices, these proposals are obviously not compatible with a long-term national policy aimed at improving family stability by encouraging marriage and discouraging markedly more unstable cohabitation.'

The average length of a marriage is 11.5 years compared with just two years for a live-in relationship.

One in four children in Britain lives in single-parent families, according to the largest survey on family life. Studies in the United States have showed these children are up to six times more likely to suffer abuse.

For a decade Labour has maintained that families of all kinds are equally good and marriage is merely a lifestyle choice.

Decades of studies have found that children of divorced or separated families, and children of single mothers, are likely to do worse at school and suffer poorer health.

As they grow up, they are more likely to fall into crime or drug abuse, to be unemployed or poor, and to become single mothers themselves.

Kyung M. Song (Seattle Times, 'Living together: a risky trial') - Contrary to what many people believe, "test driving" a relationship by living together before marriage also reduces the odds of success. The exact reasons are unclear. It may be that couples make riskier picks with a live-in partner than they would with a potential spouse. Or couples who defer marriage and opt to live together first may do so because they have trouble with commitment.

After they move in together, some couples eventually walk down the aisle as a result of inertia, not love. Undoing the entanglements of a live-in relationship can be a hassle, especially if the couple has children.

Sliding into marriage becomes "a transition without a decision". For a lot of young people, it's not a real deliberative thing.

A 2002 analysis by Jay Teachman, a sociologist at Western Washington University, found that living together increases the risk of divorce by 35 percent when those couples eventually marry.

According to Teachman, Americans are less likely to divorce if they are Catholic, have high education levels, marry someone close to their own age and don't have children before wedlock. For instance, the chances of divorce for a woman who is five or more years older than her husband is 88 percent greater than for couples without the age gap. Teachman based his calculations on more than two decades' worth of data from the National Survey of Family Growth.

Now, let us explore that what arguments some individuals have put forward against Live-in Relationships.

Muntasir Madani, Bangalore, India - The Government has gone nuts. What an irrational crap Government we are having? There was no immediate need of introducing this bill as there are so many other issues we are facing, like an economic meltdown in the making, poverty, high inflation rate, corruption, but politicians, who would prevent them from taking filmy hero steps? Maybe the Govt. thinks 'Live-in relationship' is the next biggest problem looming ahead after the possible global economic meltdown...

The Supreme Court of India has a history to go out of the way in giving judgements in favour of women, but it is understood that the Government is trying to make a law which gives compensation to a woman, in case her partner abandons her after a failed live-in relationship. It's important to understand, that if a woman gets pregnant and before delivering the baby starts living-in with a new partner, then in such a case who is liable and to be called the father of that child? In a bid to save the grace, the Government perhaps wants to have a law that might help in prevention of woman exploitation in live-in relationships, but ultimately exploiting the man.

Right now I am in a live-in relationship, so that I can understand my girl friend much better and we both can decide whether we can legalise our relationship (that is to marry). And here the Government is planning to legalise it itself.

What if we both don't get together, then I will also have to pay alimony? If they are bothered about bigamy then the rule should be specifically only directed towards married persons not on single guys.

Pete Morgan, Nashville, USA - If the man and woman (who cohabit) are not responsible enough to get married and wants to enjoy the benefits (physical and financial), then how will they ever think of supporting each other and their families as well in the time of needs such as general bad health and illness to hospitalisation.

Everybody wants freedom, but nobody wants responsibilities. And they came together but they want Live-in relationship is without responsibility.

Live-in Relationships are like Software's with 'Try before you Buy'! It's a get rich quick scheme for Women! Not comfortable with all this.

Ganesh Chintakindi, Tikabali, Kandhamal - The issue of live-in relates to moral values, but people who pose to believe in moral values and suggest others to adopt and follow them, in real life do many such things which goes against their preachings. Many people have double standards as they are talking about moral values but in reality you may know they are of very different kind and do many immoral activities behind the stage. We people are ready to do wrong (against moral values) if it does not become public, but when it gets public it becomes wrong. Then why indulge in such practices? Wrong is always wrong.

Lyla Wolf, Passau, Germany - I always advise against live-in relationships before marriage, especially anyone younger than 25! I call that playing 'house'. The older one is the more maturity gained (of course exceptions are always there). Every year makes a difference. The older has the more wisdom, even when someone thinks they know all, there is still a lot there to know now, a year later they will know more. That's why I don't think anyone younger than 25 should move too quickly because they do not know any better.

I don't understand the rush these days, everyone seems to rush into relationships that are not fulfilling, maybe it is, but they need to give it time to grow...some fear they will end up alone and have that urge to rush, some suffer from low self-esteem and want that validation/a need to feel wanted, just to give them a short-lived, false ego boost...it's truly sad. I'm 25 years old, I have had ex boyfriends' in the past that have asked me to move in with them and I have always declined. The only time I will move in with a man is when we are married! I refuse to play myself as wife and him as husband when we're not legally married. No ring, and no commitment at all! Lot of young girls don't understand that, they want to pretend to be adults and are all copying one another just to end up disappointed later. Living together does not mean a fulfilling, long-term relationship. Little do they know that love comes in time and that rushing into something that isn't meant to be is a recipe for a disaster.

Ginlalmuan Vaiphei, India - No guarantee for a woman's virginity. The people may torture the law. Such a relation is not at all possible in a country like India where women are so far suffering in the name of dowry. Don't try to imitate the Western culture too much.

The society may have matured to the level of accepting live-in relationship, but what about the status of children born out of wedlock? The law may protect the live-in couple but what about their off spring(s)? They have no legitimate status either in the eyes of law or in the eyes of the society. What happens when live-in couple splits? Is a man liable to pay for the kid's upkeep?

Alex Sebestian, Goa, India - Well, I am really not in favour of live-in relationship. I really wonder why all youth are getting so obsessed with the foreign culture that they are trying to inculcate all their moves.

The only people who go for live-in relationships are those who are financially independent. Now we might find more gold diggers around, who knows. The fact is, the real sanctity of a relationship lies in the understanding between people. When there is a price tag put, it is more like 'buying' and 'selling'.

Our country is a land of rich culture and I believe today's youth should really try to preserve its culture and tradition. Live-in relations are setting bad examples for the coming generations. People are just trying to copy the Western culture. They are not thinking that it has a lot of bad points. India is known for its culture and the culture is passed from generation to generation, so live-in relations has no value and moreover no future. In cases like live-in relationship we really don't hold any moral values. In the name of finding out the right person we are just putting ourselves into quick sand. We must learn to take good things from the West and be proud to hold our country's values. We are a nation which puts unity and relationship at the forefront.

Bilal Jafri, Chhapra, Bihar - I m not in the favour of live-in relationship. In my point of view it is not a good thing in India, because still we have faith in the institution of marriage. Marriage after all is not a contract; it's a part of our social culture. We perform marriages so that we could get a partner with whom we could survive for our life, to whom we could live, and according to Hinduism it is one of the karma of human, so that we could repay to our ancestors. And to do sex without marriage is against our values. India is known for its culture, and live-in relationship will only spoil the situation. It will hamper the feeling of sincerity and responsibility. The persons who are in favour of live-in relationship say that there is not a commitment in their life, they are free , there is no responsibility, Then to those persons let me ask one thing "Would you have gone to school and completed your studies, if you had not been forced into it?" Of course we wouldn't have. Now let's grow up a little and assume if you got your salary with your boss giving you the option of attending office at your own will, What will happen? We all know the answer. Why does that happen? This is human tendency when given an option we always go for the easier one. So commitment is the foundation of any relation, if there is no foundation we cannot have any construction, building a relation. Let us suppose we still feel we should go for a live-in relation, have you ever thought what happens if one of you gets involved with the other and the other is just not serious in the relation. People who get attached with their pets can't live without them, and here we are exploring and talking about human attachment.

Hence live-in relationship is not a right move. It is a major threat for our culture because even till today, in Indian culture, relationship between opposite sex before marriage is considered to be a sin. Live-in relationship will only help corrupting of mind and it will darken the future of youths who are the future of the country.

Hikaru Ito, Tokyo, Japan - It's a corruption from the Western culture and quite alien to our own culture. It strongly deserves to be discouraged if we want to save our society.

Live-in relationship is a kind of public services particularly for the male genders, offered by the women of the society. It's a kind of charity. A woman offering this kind of relationship is similar to the status of a Prostitute. Would you like your sister living in with someone and having sex before marriage?

Brandon Miller, Fayette, Alabama - I think it is not just to blame only men for it. If men do have a relation before marriage, it has to be with a woman who herself is not married (unless otherwise), so I feel it should be thought over from both sides and if at all it should be blamed, then both should be blamed for it. The only way to stop such a thing is to take a conscious decision for yourself, whether you are doing is right or wrong. Otherwise, that day will not be far when no man will trust a woman and no woman will trust a man as well to whom they are getting married. The thread of trust will be broken before the marriage and marriage itself will lose its significance.

Chandrasekhar (Legal Consultant), Hyderabad, India - I don't know what happens in elite families which are settled in US / UK and other advanced countries. I belong to Middie class Hindu family. More than 75 percent of the Indian population either belongs to poor or middle class societies that are governed by values and traditions of our country that have been existed since times immemorial.

We don't treat 'Car' and 'Wife' at par, because if we don't like a car we will refuse it to buy and purchase another one. We cannot give the same treatment to wife. Our culture does not allow relationships to depend on the whims and fancies of the people involved, say, he does not know how to dance in parties, I will give divorce to him...that kind of reckless attitude we do not encourage in our culture.

It is not only in relationship between wife and husband, in many other human relationships you find some kind of inconvenience. Say in a relationship between father and son, mother and daughter, father and daughter...in so many other relationships also we find conflicts and inconvenience. Do we throw away our mothers and fathers like we throw away our children and wives giving divorce?

Marriage is not for promoting 'material interests' in India, it is for practicing spirituality and goodness.

We cannot get rid of relationships as easily as it happens in Western countries. We have to accept good and bad of our life partner, and strive to achieve the spiritual goals. That is why people still have strong emotional bonds in India.

There is no question of a girl asking the guy or guy asking questions to girl about her virginity. In fact, we view it as an insult to our self-respect to be asked such questions. No girl who respects herself can tolerate such questions. It is all based on trust and goodness the relationship gets fructified.

There are instances of guys, who married very innocent and soft natured women brought up in good and decent families and harassed them mentally "Why don't you come to pubs and discos?", "Why don't you dance with my friends?", "Why don't you sexually please my friend?" "You tell me about your past sexual fantasies....on whom you had crush?"...."Why don't you booze?"...etc., because they want to remain in "hot mood" always.

We have also seen what impact these kinds of guys are making on our society. We are making our best efforts to prevent our girls from falling victim to that kind of trends.

Western lifestyle goes with the notion, "Everybody in the world is bad, I shall not trust anyone for his goodness and depend on anyone except my own money". Indian lifestyle goes with the notion, "Everyone in the world is good like me, if I keep practicing goodness and doing good to people, everybody else will do the same for me".

Our culture, values and traditions are not so easy to understand. It is true our culture has to change with times, but simultaneously we should not forget to preserve and explore what purpose the old values, traditions and customs serve.

Hari Balasubramanium, Chidambaram, Tamil Nadu - I thought that people enter into live-in relationship because they want flexibility and want to avoid hassles of marriage. Now getting benefits without getting responsibilities of marriage is clearly not fair. I accept law which can permit live-in relationships to be certified so help them book hotel room or rent a house, and domestic abuse is simply law against violence, but maintenance is like double benefit for 'other' woman. And in such cases we seem to forget that the 'other' woman has choice, and entered into live-in relationship and avoided marriage knowing what it means and what it doesn't. Worst tragedy is laws like this, and the year 2007 modified Domestic Violence Law, are so heavily biased against men, is that most uses are by women to harass men, because those who really need protection, and there are lots of them, don't really know the law or are too constrained by society.

Wajeeh Qadir, Aligarh, Uttar Pradesh - I am against this system. May be, at the time of enjoying life, it will be pretty interesting. But, at the end part, there will be no one to support.

Our Indian culture doesn't allow this type of relationship. Youngsters, who are attracted to such relationships, have to think first, what will be the future of this immoral and affectionless relationship? This relationship is based solely on lust and when the lust ends, the relation snaps.

There will be problems for both the partners. If a child is expected as a result, then what will be the future of that child? Definitely, we have to oppose this system and the Government should not encourage such type of things, which put a bad mark on Indian culture.

Pam Sorooshian, Bacharach, Germany - I don't think it is wrong, but I think people should really be committed to one another before doing so. I think it ruins most relationships because you've not actually got to know that person thoroughly and know that it is them that you want to be with. When you move in with someone, you are there with him/her all the time and there is no "games" anymore or pretending. You can put on your makeup, or style your hair but you still see her/him when you wake up and when you're not all gussied up.

I unfortunately moved in with my boyfriend of only 4 months, and we stayed together for 2 1/2 years but broke up, and we haven't been happy since we started living together. We just became content and comfortable with one another so we stayed. Neither of us was actually enjoying the relationship. In fact, right after we'd moved in we stopped having sex and everything was lost, and we were so young... so it didn't make sense. To make the story short, I think people should really do this at least without knowing one another whether how young or old they are before they make the decision of moving in together.

Udipti Sarkar, Dryden, Ontario - If people are not ready to get married, let them not. But making the web will get more tangled by laws like these, you people are mocking at legal wives like me. Am I fool or stupid enough to marry? Is life all about staying together without sharing any responsibilities? I wonder which dirty woman on the first instance will opt to become a mistress, spoiling the wife's rights.

I have no issues with young upper society living together; they don't get married, because they don't want to. But now they want to get the rights of the legal wives. How funny and hypocritical. If rights matters so much, why don't they get married?

Newspapers, especially times online is hell bent over convincing everybody that "Open marriages" is nothing wrong and in fact it is very beneficial and all...bla, bla, bla...

We all are talking very loudly about individual freedom. I have seen people religiously arguing that Hindu culture encloses such things and hence there is nothing wrong in India adapting this stuff.

My issue is not with live-in relationships, but in their sick hypocrisy that they don't want to get married, but want to get all rights of husbands and wives.

I really don't understand why people opt not to get married even when they have kids. Strange! If the society accepts them I guess they don't care much like in some countries. In India you won't see couples having kids without marriage and living a normal life. But you see it in bigamous relationships. I am sure in some cases women go in for it with open eyes and wonder why they should choose such a life. May be they are already abandoned by their partners and need someone else. I know a case like this, a maid who started living with a rickshaw driver knowing he had a wife. She told me that living alone as an abandoned woman was tough and also not safe. I personally would not judge anyone who makes this decision. Who knows what their circumstances are? But overall the concept of living-in is cowardliness.

Arijeet Sahai, Leeds, United Kingdom - All posters complaining about aping the West should simply wake up from their deluded state. The Indian value systems have been trashed long time ago and there is hardly anything left to ape.

But this issue is different. The Indian marriage system is rotten and over legalised. Any male that enters into a marriage in India is taking a serious risk with umpteen number of draconian laws stacked against him. While getting on with it is impossible getting out of it is prohibitively expensive. The Indian legislative system promotes relationship under duress.

So no wonder that marriages are becoming less preferred and in the medium term, as more awareness about the pitfalls emerges, people will continue to shun marriages. Live-in was the fallback option - it offered everything a marriage offered without the bondages and lopsided legislative threats.

Make marriages less of bondage by removing unwanted high handed laws.... That is the only way to encourage marriages - Legislation is and will never be a long term substitute to values - Unfortunately in India uneducated legislators don't get it.

One thing has to be remembered that most of the live-ins are among Hindu couples. Muslims are governed by Sharia and consider it 'Haraam'. Hindus again are covered by Hindu Marriage Act which needs to be reviewed. Many Hindu couples live their entire married life without a legal document showing them as man and wife. Succession issues are difficult even for legally married wives. Live-in under the Hindu Marriage Act and also the Sharia act is illegal and I don't think it can ever be legalised as such.

A live-in is good in the sense that partners can live as long as they please and leave when they get bored. It is entered into for social security and safe sex without the add-ons of married life. There should be no complaints as it provides mutual benefits. One should not complain after breaking up.

Amit Bose, Bishnupur, WB - I believe that if this law is passed, men will think twice before entering into a live-in relationship. Live-in relationships are in practice because the couple thinks that they are not bound to their partners by any law. But the law might change this perception.

Again, keeping a second wife might also not be as lucrative. People do all such things because there are no legal actions attached to them. The moment you attach the word "law" to it, the thing becomes graver.

If a man has to support the live-in, he will hesitate to get into a relationship. About how it will affect women I don't know. If society does not except her even if she has financial security, then I think women may not be inclined that much. Now whether social sanction will improve if the law changes, well I don't know because we have so many laws against dowry but still society accepts dowry givers. In fact it is possible that society will hate the other woman even more as she is now a financial threat.

Xylene Gandhi, Ozhukarai, Pondicherry - The cohabitation, whether legalised or not, is not going to make any sense and will always pose danger for the society at large. I don't think that this is going to deter men from cheating on their wife because it's not the money that matter to them. It's only his honesty and morality that would make a difference.

Live-in relationship is not Indian Culture. People will be in deep shit in such relationship. Will you allow or suggest your Sister or Daughter to go for "live-in relationship". No doubt it is personal choice of two adults and no one has the right to interfere. If the children are born out of this relationship, they would be the worst hit if the relationship ends. And also does the law classify the time period a couple should live together to get compensation?

Nazneen O' Saherwala, Rawalpindi, Pakistan - Islam allows four wives. Legalisation of Live-in relationships in India means Islamisation of a Hindu law. Are you ready for it? Are you ready to accept a second woman as a legal wife? Any religion it may be, but sooner or later it is the woman who has to pay the price. So, before legalising this unethical and immoral trend of living-in, the Supreme Court of India should think twice.

Atul Nandwani, Pune, India - Legalising the 'Live-in' will add to many woes. It will be a license for prostitution. Moreover, the whole purpose of marriage was pro-creation, which will be dead. As due to legal abortion, millions of lives are killed. So now legally people who live-in, will kill innocent unborn babies. Moreover the youths are told to have free sex, no need of marriage to stay together, when fed-up live or ditch and go, move on. The whole society will be destroyed. Why do we have to follow the West? Smoking, Drugs, Pornography, Sex, Marital laws, Alcohol..., they all are fed up with it. Our Nation has a rich heritage and culture. Why do we need to follow the West? We are a wonderful nation; we do not need to borrow from any other society. Even today there are children, who respect their parents and elders. Even today we stay in joint families. Even today we wait for proposals to get married. Let's not be a slave to the West. Let's not legalise prostitution. It will help more anti-social elements, and evil will win its battle against family values.

So, there is a total 'No' to its legalisation. Live-in is a bye pass to responsibilities linked with marriage, especially social duties. Live-in is an individualist strategy for personal benefits, mostly at the cost of social strategies. A society is a collective responsibility. Individualistic tendencies conflict with collective social strategies, development, and goal.

Maira Malik, Mississauga - It is very painful to know that after targeting the minority religions, and then the minority communities, now the politicians are turning towards the young who forms a major vote bank. By sanctioning the live-in relationship, the present set of Indian politicians are dismantling the very structure of Indian culture, which every religion and caste in India follow sincerely. The live-in relationships in the West have resulted in many cases of psychiatric problems, and now India is going to follow. What will be the status of the child born out of such relationship? Will this child get the love and affection of grand-parents and other family members? Are these children not going to grow as the ones with disturbed childhood?

The basic question is why is it necessary to have such a relationship legalised? Marriage is an institution where you need to adjust to each other, learn to give and take. It teaches tolerance to the young couple. Even in the West, children born out of such relations look down on themselves when in a company of children who have legally married parents.

Vikas Mahlawat, Jaipur, Rajasthan - Legalising 'Live-in' is one more act of harassing the 'Men At The Hands Of Females'. As if the dowry law was not enough.

"NO" It will not solve the problem of the deserving and genuine females who are suffering.

As the females living in these relations are mostly educated above 18 years of age and from the Urban / Metros areas, considering themselves as modern, who consider sleeping with men as not a big deal, always of the opinion that they can understand everything good or bad for themselve, then why the Fuss now? And get the protection behind an act of law. Live-in relation is considered by these females as a means of expressing their independence and modernity. These females have decent paying jobs.

Anon, Croydon, U.K. – Live-in relationships? What a shit? When in today's date most of the people are ending their married life also with a divorce, we are talking about a relationship without marriage? If you favour the other way then just think for a while what will you feel when you come to know that your mother or your wife had a live-in relationship with someone else before marriage? Will you be able to accept the truth that someone else has also touched your wife's or mother's skin? I think no man can support that. So, if you have this feeling, don't your wives' have the right to have the same feeling? At least think once before entering into any such relationship.

Perneet Shergill, Toronto, Canada - When two adults choose live-in relationship as their way of life they are not able to avoid sexual relationship (as known in the most cases). It results in "Sex Before Marriage". Even they are not able to continue this relationship for whole life (because they are aware that when they reach 40's, 50's or 60's they will need a family to look after them). They have to return to "Marriage

Institution". And if they keep their past "live-in relationship" secret to their spouse they will deceive them. It results in "Break of Trust" (Indian Husband / Wife hardly accepts their spouse's "Sex Before Marriage" fact). It can endanger their marriage also. So it is not according to the Indian culture and tradition.

I agree that it is not always a bad idea for a couple to live together before getting married, but I don't think that marriage involves more legal problems. I think the opposite is true. A lot of live-in couples have endless problems when it comes to ownership.

Rohan Dadwal, Bilaspur, H.P., India - The reason why Maharashtra Government has legalised live-in relationships is because women can demand maintenance from their live-in partners and the men can be screwed up. If the law says that a live-in female can become a wife, she can claim property rights of the husband. Then what is difference between a wife in a married relationship and a live-in partner?

What is the purpose of a live-in relationship? Most people in the West go for a live-in because they don't want the hassles of a married life. To put it better, getting married is easier than getting a separation or divorce. When a couple gets divorced, the man takes the brunt as he has to shell out huge alimony, maintenance etc. and invariably he will be sued for domestic violence. So, the marriage rate, post-feminism in the West has come down to 50 percent because most men know the consequences of marriage as marriage is a trap for men - they can neither continue with their unreasonable partners nor can they get a divorce since divorce becomes expensive.

If women in live-in relationships are considered as wives, then, why have live-in relationships at all? You can as well go for a married life. Don't get carried away by the news that live-in relationships are recognised. That is just for the men to pay a hefty alimony and give property rights to live-in female partners. So from now on, women can live-in a hundred times in their lives and become extremely wealthy.

Girls today are flirting around a lot (technology has added to that) and this will destroy the moral fabric of India. Because women have the responsibility of supporting humanity and 'NO' man can ever do this. They were the moral custodians and the day they are liberated from that most important role, society will plunge into chaos.

Who says that in a marriage man always dominates? It is always the women who have been dominating - men do the riskiest of jobs in the world, pay heavy tax to the Government, pay alimony and sacrifice their lives at the border.

The proposed new legislation would rather discourage live-in relationships since there wouldn't be any difference between a live-in and a marriage. The new law, which gives live-in a legal sanctity, would now be a very convenient way for women to extort money from the men. You guys end up paying maintenance and half of your property is spent for having lived with her for few years. She then goes and hooks on to another man and does the same for another few years. So for men, live-in becomes a great liability just as marriage is a liability today, worse than going to a prostitute since you pay a few thousands for a few hours.

Guys, if there are no rules at all in our society, as you want it to be, society will plunge into chaos. The baby which your live-in lady is carrying may not be yours. Still, you will have to take care of that and when she decides to call it a day, you will end up with paying alimony and half your property. Do you want that to happen? Why a ditched man cannot claim anything from his live-in female (if she is rich and earning)?

Sreeniwas, Nasik, Maharashtra, India - I am shocked at Government of Maharashtra's unnecessary dabbling in our social structure, which has roots in Indian culture. Such an action on part of the Government is totally unwarranted and harmful for social stability. Marriage Institution has certain sanctity in Indian psyche and has special significance in our lives. Government's action in legalising live-in relationships will subvert the social order and shall lead to chaos and social instability. It will be foolish of us to copy Western customs in our society blindly, which will harm our social fabric. Instead we need to inculcate Western characteristics such as for instance freedom of thought, cleanliness, innovation, creativity etc.

I don't understand as to why the Government is seized of this issue, when far more important issues like education, unemployment, burgeoning population, development of infrastructure including power generation etc. need to be focused upon. The Government needs to give far more attention to population control rather than enacting legislations in matters such as live-in relationships, which are not and should not be on its list of its priorities at all. And as above said, legalising live-in relations will have damaging effect on social stability and hence is worthy of forthright rejection.

If the Government is thinking of projecting itself as a 'Modern State with Modern Thinking' by such enactment, it's wrong. Will it legalise a man and a woman living together and thereby provid certain rights to the woman, in spite of one of them having wife or husband respectively from whom legal divorce has not been obtained? If the answer is yes, then marriage as well as divorce will lose meaning and the rights of the woman in live-in relationship will encroach upon the rights of the woman who is legally married to the man. This will be the total injustice to the married woman. Hence, if at all any legislation is to be enacted regarding live-in relationships, it must specify that, when a man is already married, his living-in relationship with another woman will not be covered under the enactment until he has obtained a legally valid divorce from his legal wife. In addition, it must also provide that, the living relationship can be considered only from the date from which legal divorce comes into effect. The minimum period of live-in relations for the woman involved in the relationship to be able to get its benefits as her rights will also have to be specified in the enactment.

It is also possible that, some unscrupulous elements may misuse the provisions of such a legislation to malign some individuals by distorting facts of the case so as to reap financial benefits.

Last but not the least, this legislation need not be given any importance in terms of priority by Central Government for clearance. There are many far more urgent issues before the Central Government and all State Governments as well to act on them. I am really shocked as to how Government of Maharashtra finds time to even think on the issue of live-in relationships at the present juncture when far more pressing and important issues about citizens' lives need focused attention and satisfactory solution.

Moreover, too much of individual freedom is harmful to the society, to its stability. We see that too much of freedom of expression in a democratic set up like ours leads to irresponsible outbursts, misguided agitations from those who are basically aggressive and vociferous by nature. There is always a necessity of checks and counterchecks to keep things in balance. Individual freedoms, if it is exercised in an irresponsible manner, can lead to social anarchy, which needs to be avoided.

Again, some have put forth a view that, Indian culture has roots in Kamasutra or something akin to that. We must bear in mind that, culture and tradition have evolved over time; even Gods have evolved over time. As on today, Indian society has accepted and respects Marriage Institution as sacrosanct forming the basis for stability of our society. We, Indians, sons of this ancient land, worship Lord Rama who had only one wife, although that was not customary in his times. This is the ideal we cherish even today. Government should not destroy it. Before enacting the proposed law, it can have a referendum on contents of the same as the law will have far reaching effects on our society.

Simplifying divorce laws to enable quicker outcomes for incompatible couples is a better idea instead of legalising live-in relationships. It is my view that, the proposed law can be misused with the result that, more number of women will suffer due to deceit. Women must strongly oppose its enactment.

Robert Chelaiyyah, Washington D.C. - It is preposterous. It's happening in Maharashtra, India, really unthinkable and totally unacceptable! Politicians were perceived to be sans intellect but now it seems that they have gone morally bankrupt completely. What is being proposed in the name of the honour of ladies is a shame.

Look, what has happened to American (rather all Western) society. They admire Indians the most for family bonds and values and here we are! These politicians are trying to dismantle the very edifice of our society. They are playing with fire! This is certainly not progressive thinking. It is downright retrograde.

I think this is probably the worst thing we can accept for our beautiful Indian culture. Living in US for so many years I have seen the downside of these relationships and also the mental status of the people after they break-up. It is easy as you are not forced to follow the marriage institution laws but there are so many good things about marriage. The family, the tradition, the values and most important is security. 'NOT' all marriages fail. I strictly think that the Government of India needs to work more on the rural uplifting and infrastructure of the nation then focussing on these concepts for total destruction.

Lovelle Grayson, Merton, London, U.K. - People who are afraid of commitment try the live-in relationship, I believe. Otherwise what is wrong in marriage when anyway, you want to live together?

A lot of live-in couples have endless problems when it comes to ownership. For instance, if a live-in couple moves to a new house, and they split the cost both ways, only one partner can be the registered owner of the property. If the couple splits up on bad terms - which are not a rare occurrence

- it will be very easy and perfectly legal for the registered owner to sell the property and run away with all the cash.

I completely disagree with the idea that marriage is unattractive to young people because they fear and can't handle commitment or faithfulness. I think the reason is far less simplistic than that. Young people aren't bums. They work hard to go to university, and it has become normal to get more than one degree. They have a lot on their mind, and are more driven and committed than ever. Young people commit themselves to an education and to a career, rather than to marriage. Demographers have noticed that in the past decade people are getting married and having children much later than before, because young people swear allegiance to other things, and not because they are not committed at all.

Vrinda Kochar, New Delhi, India - Before we regulate the live-in relationships, I think there is more need to regulate marriage. With honour killing, dowry deaths and the like being a norm in the society, I don't think the society is regulated in any manner. It's totally up to the individuals to opt, rather than trying to ensure "sanctity" to avoid animal instinct in a so called regulated society, which failed to ensure the sanctity of marriage as an institution.

The **Pages from Australia** also show the grim reality of Living Together and the following article appeared in the Sydney Morning Herald 12 April 2003, written by Bettina Arndt.

"Living together sounds modern and mature, but it often masks a lack of commitment that can cruel women's chances of having children."

"I never expected to be 41, on my own and childless. Being single is not so terrible. You can always find a companion and I have many other good things in my life. But I always wanted to be a mum and am upset about the possibility I won't have kids. That really hurt me."

This is Alison, now happily working in a bookshop after a successful career in the finance industry. She's one of a growing number of women likely to miss out on having children. More than a quarter of today's young women will never be mothers, the Australia Bureau of Statistics estimates.

Most women still want children, but up to 10 percent of couples are infertile often due to age-related problems and large numbers are missing out because of the hazards of modern partnering patterns.

One of the main reasons Australian women, particularly better-educated women, end up childless is they don't have the right man at the right time. More than a quarter of Australian women in those critical years between 35 and 39 don't have partners, and about a fifth have never married, according to research by Bob Birrell at Monash University, using data from the latest census. (Not all of them, however, are childless a quarter of women in this age group with degrees, and more than half of those without post-secondary qualifications, are single mothers.)

Research from the **Australian Institute of Family Studies** (AIFS) shows, that 13 percent of the un-partnered childless group have been married, but they separated before having children. Many more experience another type of relationship breakdown a live-in relationship that splits up.

James Sweet, a sociology professor at the University of Wisconsin, dubbed these relationships "pre-marital divorces", which implies an easy way out for relationships destined not to last. In the long term, these relationships may carry heavy penalties, especially for women.

These relationships are scrutinised by international researchers, who have observed that in most Western countries in recent years, cohabitation has replaced marriage as the first "live-in" relationship. And, whereas these relationships once led to marriage, this is now less likely. The AIFS has found that two-thirds of cohabiting couples married within five years in the early '70s. The rate in the '90s was only 40 percent. A further 20 percent remained living together and the rest broke up.

The result is many women hit their '40s being unmarried and childless, often after spending time in a number of live-in relationships. Living together may cruel women's chances of mating in time to have children. Adding to the problem is the fact that most women, particularly educated women, don't even consider marriage until their late '20s, which leaves precious few years for achieving family goals.

A woman who spends too long in cohabiting relationships begins to incur what economists call "opportunity costs", explains Barbara Dafoe Whitehead (an author). "Each year she spends in a cohabiting relationship that doesn't 'work out' is one less year available to invest in a successful search for a life partner . . . While she is waiting for Mr. Not Ready or Mr. Maybe or Mr. Someday to make up his mind, she is missing opportunities to meet other potential partners for whom she may be ready and willing to marry."

The average age for a woman to marry for the first time is now 27. The time crunch is really on. The Sydney fertility expert Robert Jansen warned in the Australian Medical Journal recently of steady falls in success rates for IVF (In Vitro Fertilisation - the joining of a woman's egg and a man's sperm in a laboratory dish.) from the age of 33.

Jill, a Sydney preschool teacher, spent six years with her Mr. Maybe. She met him when she was 35. It was the children issue that brought them unstuck. He'd been married before and had grown-up children of his own. Only now does Jill acknowledge how much she glossed over his reluctance to add to his family. They married after four years of living together and tried to conceive, but the marriage was quickly on the rocks. At the time of her first critical ovulation, Jill found herself alone. Her husband was suddenly absent on an unnecessary interstate trip.

Now 46, single and childless, Jill realises the timing of this failed relationship was crucial. "If I'd made that mistake at 28 or 29, I'd still have had those other years." And she's also aware that she didn't push hard enough to find out where her husband really stood on the children issue. "My husband didn't want to do it, but he wanted to keep me," she concludes.

One characteristic of live-in relationships is that the couples often avoid the hard questions, Whitehead says. "People can slide into living together, without any serious discussion or mutual understanding as to its meaning, purpose or likely duration . . . As a consequence; cohabitation-as-courtship can contribute to confusion, misunderstanding, miscommunication and faulty assumptions. It is easy for a couple to decide to live together and, at the same time, harbour very different expectations for the relationship."

Given this ambiguity, it becomes easy for a woman to think the relationship is progressing towards marriage while her partner is content with the status quo. Gemma, 28, is a Melbourne yoga teacher. She's always known she wanted to have children and would have been happy to start her family in her early '20s. But issues of marriage and children were never raised in the four-year live-in relationship she had at the time. "I never talked to him about it. I think I knew deep down that he was always less committed and to make my desires so overt would have pushed him away."

Andrew Cargill is a Melbourne psychotherapist who has worked with women in live-in relationships. "Many are so anxious, they don't even dare voice or fully acknowledge their own expectations for fear he will withdraw, scamper, end the relationship." He says it isn't uncommon for these relationships to drift on for years in this uncertainty an uncertainty he feels suits many men. "They feel they have a lot to lose. Our culture has encouraged a hedonistic lifestyle and they are reluctant to give it up."

The result is many men embrace live-in relationships as the answer to all their dreams. In 2002, Whitehead and David Popenoe, who are co-directors of the National Marriage Project at Rutgers University, conducted focus groups in which they asked men aged 25 to 33 why they weren't married. Their answers included: easy access to sex; cohabitation provided the benefits of marriage without the downside; they wanted to avoid divorce and its financial risks; they wanted to enjoy the single life as long as they could; they wanted to wait till they were older to have children; they feared marriage would require too many changes and compromises; they were waiting for their soul mate; they faced few social pressures to marry; they were reluctant to marry a woman with children; and they wanted a house first.

Many of these answers gel with what Cargill has been hearing. But he also finds that many men are unimpressed by what they have seen of marriage and family life. "They've looked at their parents' marriage and said: 'I don't want to go there'. They haven't seen their fathers as being all that satisfied with being married, or being a father." It's hardly surprising young men are nervous many have seen fathers end up divorced and alienated from their children.

Also, some men simply find themselves in live-in relationships that aren't fulfilling. Steve, a Sydney pilot, spent two years in such a relationship in his late '20s. "I was losing interest but I knew she wasn't," he says. It got a bit scary towards the end. 'You don't like someone to keep having the wrong impression. You've got to either spell it out or you do it the soft way and ease yourself out of the situation." They never talked about it. He eased himself out by taking a job interstate. Now 54, he has just married. His former live-in partner is in her early 40s, married and childless.

But there's also a broader issue, affecting both young men and women namely that children are no longer seen as rewarding. "Many young people don't see children as bringing something into your life. Children are seen as taking something from you," says Cargill. The research bears him out. Surveys show that far fewer people see children as important to life satisfaction. In 1971, two-thirds of people agreed that "a woman is only really fulfilled when she becomes a mother". By 1991, this figure had dropped to 7 percent, according to research by AIFS and the Australian National University.

The reason for this shift, according to Whitehead, lies in efforts to encourage girls to aim for independence by acquiring a good education and a successful career. What she calls "the girl project" has been an astonishing success but, in the process, the traditional goals of marriage and children have been denigrated or relegated to a distant someday that often never arrives.

Virginia Haussegger, a news presenter for ABC TV in Canberra, says: "The message I heard was that to have children and marry young was a cop-out. Those women miss out if they do that. I always used to say: "I'm never having children." "In the year 2002, Haussegger had written newspaper articles claiming women of her generation were duped into believing that satisfaction lay in having rich careers, with the result that many are now childless, alone or drifting in "ambiguous, uncommitted" relationships.

"None of our purple-clad feminist mothers thought to tell us the truth about the biological clock . . . the one that would eventually reach exploding point inside us . . . None of our mothers thought to warn us that we would need to stop, take time out and learn to nurture our partnerships and relationships. Or, if they did, we were running too fast to hear it," she wrote.

Although Haussegger's articles had been greeted with sympathy and support, she also had attracted considerable hostility, laced with a sense of betrayal. "How very petulant of you, I would expect as much from my 15-year-old," one woman responded. "Stop bleating . . . None of us has it all," said another. "Some feminists don't have babies and live with that choice because it was just that: a choice," said a third.

But it's often a misguided choice arrived at through distorted messages about life satisfaction, says Cargill, who notes the irony that "therapists have long worked with men in their '40s who arrive at a disillusionment because their careers didn't end up fulfilling them".

AIFS research shows that nearly half of all people who start out not wanting children end up changing their minds. But, with infertility increasing so sharply with age, the change may come too late for many.

Yet, for every single woman unhappy at missing out on marriage and children, there is another quite content. Like Suzi, 48, a Sydney physiotherapist: "I never felt I wanted to live in a couple situation forever. I find it very stifling. It's unlikely I will do it now unless it is an exceptional sort of person and a very big house," she says. "I always knew I didn't want to spend my whole life wiping noses, cooking dinners and all that stuff. Marriage is a so much better deal for men." Suzi has spent time in two live-in relationships. She was always the one who wanted out. "They wanted more commitment than I could give."

So there are women, as well as men, shying away from long-term commitment, and there are also couples living together in long-term relationships who share a mutual lack of interest in marriage or children. The AIFS has finished research, which has found that fewer than half of couples who have lived together for more than five years expect to marry. Other AIFS research suggests many of them are committed to a long-term relationship and have no interest in tying the knot.

Indeed, increasing numbers are having children in such relationships. But this is far less common for educated women: among 30 to 49 year olds who have never married and who live alone, only 13 per cent have had children from live-in relationships. This compares with 59 percent of those who haven't finished school, according to data from the Household, Income and Labour Dynamics in Australia Survey (conducted for the Commonwealth Department of Family and Community Services).

But within that group of live-in couples will be people whose low expectations are based on problems in the relationship, or simply the knowledge that their partner isn't in it for the long haul. And, while men's more leisurely body clock means they can afford to dally, women seeking marriage and children do not have that luxury.

As Whitehead says, "we've come a long way from the time when the crowning achievement of a woman's life was her youthful marriage. But, along with the support that exists for women's success in education and work, they must also be encouraged to achieve the equally important goals of commitment and children, by being more intentional about their private lives. If they are to find partners by their late '20s and early '30s, they can afford to waste very little time away from the main game."

Sandra Dodd, Sydney, Australia – Marriage of course has upper hand as to live-in relationship. What a wife can do for her husband, no live-in partner or mistress can do for her man. I am against changing definition of a wife. Wife can never be equal to a live-in partner or mistress, whatever you call it. Husband gets respect because of wife and vice versa.

In live-ins and mistress relationships, you do not want to take responsibilities. Legalising this would force to take such financial responsibilities. I think wife should be provided maximum benefits if marriages breaks up. Live-ins may get few but mistress none at all. It's not good for the society to encourage live-ins by giving equal status as wife. How much respect children of such 'arrangement' will get? That's the real question to ask them.

9

The Final Verdict

The Final Verdict

Actually the whole world is divided over the issue of Cohabitation and particularly the Indians talked a lot about the issue, before and specially after the passing of the crucial judgement by the Supreme Court of India on March 23, 2010, in the South Indian film actress Khushboo's case. The legalising of 'Live-in Relationship' has not gone down the throats of most of the Indians, but there are many who were and still are in the favour of the concept of cohabitation.

People are quoted here as per their pre and post judgement comments and views are incorporated to understand the feelings and emotions of the masses.

The agreeing and disagreeing persons are not from any particular region or religion but the people from all walks of life have come forward with their ideas.

Before proceeding with the comments of the people we must learn what the Apex Court of India had to say in its historical judgement which can tear the social fabric to the core if the concept of 'Living-in Together' is not understood and handled with responsibly.

Live-in relationship, pre-marital sex not an offence: Supreme Court of India

Cohabitation is not an offence but a 'Right to Life', says India's Apex Court

To be or not to be in live-in relationship is the most debated question after Supreme Court's recent observation on the issue of live-in relationship.

The Supreme Court of India threw its weight behind live in relationships on March 23, 2010, observing that for a man and woman in love, to live together is part of the right to life, and not a "criminal offence". The Supreme Court has endorsed the right of unmarried couples to live together in a case involving Ms. Khusboo (a South Indian noted actress by profession) accused of outraging public decency.

Few years back the actress was in news for her radical comments on pre-marital sex. She had then remarked that in the present times a man should not expect his wife to be virgin before marriage. The remarks made by her stirred controversy in a conservative society, where pre-marital sex is still a cultural taboo.

Some Tamil nationalist political groups accused the actress of making derogatory and obscene remarks against Tamil culture. Several cases have been filed against her across Tamil Nadu in various courts under different sections of the Indian penal code.

Her statement stirred up a hornet's nest. Daggers were drawn against her; the moralists in the society ran after her blood. They condemned her views vehemently. She had triggered outrage for saying that there was nothing wrong with sex before marriage had approached and took her legal battle to the Apex Court (Supreme Court) after the Madras High Court in 2008 dismissed her plea for quashing the criminal cases filed against her throughout Tamil Nadu.

If found guilty, she had to face imprisonment or a fine.

"When two adult people want to live together what is the offence? Does it amount to an offence? Living together is not an offence. It cannot be an offence," a three judge bench of Chief Justice K.G. Balakrishnan, Deepak Verma and B.S. Chauhan observed.

In an observation that will cheer votaries of pre-marital sex and live-in partners, the Supreme Court opined that a man and woman living together without marriage cannot be construed as an offence.

The Supreme Court has gone a step further observing that pre-marital sex between two adults is no offence; the law does not prohibits the consenting adults if they opt to go for pre-marital sex.

The Apex Court made the observation while reserving its judgement on a special leave petition filed by Ms. Kushboo seeking to quash more than 20 criminal cases filed against her by Tamil activist groups, which accused her of corrupting young minds by promoting pre-marital sex after she allegedly endorsed pre-marital sex by telling the magazines in various interviews on Aids awareness, in which she stressed the importance of protected sex in 2005 saying that "no educated man would expect his (bride) to be a virgin". She said it was fine for girls to have pre-marital sex, but they must take precautions to prevent pregnancy and sexually transmitted diseases. All these bold statements drew anger and protests in the Southern India's Tamil Nadu State.

The actress said the cases against her violated her fundamental right to freedom of speech and expression.

The judges, while reserving judgement on her appeal, challenged the lawyers of the complainants to produce evidence supporting their argument.

"The scenario is highly unlikely in this age of the Internet, when we do not know what our children are doing or where they are going or what pornography site they are watching," they said.

The judges grilled the counsel for some of the complainants in the case and repeatedly stressed that the perceived immoral activities cannot be branded as offence.

The lawyer for one of the complainants argued that her comments in 2005 misled the young. The argument of the counsel was that her comments allegedly endorsing pre-marital sex would adversely affect the minds of young people leading to decay in moral values and country's ethos.

"When two adult people want to live together, what is the offence and under which section? Living together is not an offence. It is a right to life," the judges said apparently referring to Article 21 which granted Right to Life and Liberty as a Fundamental Right.

The Supreme Court further said the views expressed by Ms. Khusboo were personal. When Khusboo's counsel Pinky Anand read out a portion of her interview to a fortnightly magazine whose translated version in a Tamil newspaper created pandemonium and led to filing of 23 complaint cases against her all over the country, the court wanted to know from the complainants as to what was so abhorrent in her view.

"How does it concern you? We are not bothered. At the most it is a personal view. How is it an offence? Under which provision of the law?" the bench asked the counsel.

The Apex Court further asked the complainants to produce evidence to show if any girls eloped from their homes after the said interview.

"How many homes have been affected can you tell us," the Bench asked while enquiring whether the complainants had daughters. When the response was in the negative, they shot back, "Then, how are you adversely affected?"

The court ruled then that a man and a woman, having lived together for a long time, would be presumed to have been married, unless it was rebutted by convincing evidence.

"If living together is an offence, then the first complaint should be filed against the Supreme Court, because we have permitted living together," the court said. It was referring to a 2006 judgement in which the Supreme Court directed the administration and police across the country to protect runaway couples from harassment, and to initiate action against those resorting to violence.

In 2008, the court ruled that long-term, live-in relationships should be validated as marriages and that children born out of such relationships would no longer be considered "illegitimate".

Referring to Hindu mythology, the Apex Court pointed out to substantiate its point that even Lord Krishna and Radha were live-in lovers.

A reference by the Supreme Court to Hindu Gods' pair Radha-Krishna's relationship, however, has raised eyebrows of the many. Voices of protest are loud and full of animosity especially from the quarters of Vishwa Hindu Parishad (VHP). The Honourable Supreme Court of India now faces difficult emotional fallout. It's very derogatory, they say, to bring God into live-in relationship controversy. Lord Krishna was only 12 years of age when he left Vrindavan (his native place); his relation with Goddess Radha was in his childhood days. How could a child be in erotic live-in relationship?

The complexities of live-in relationships

The Supreme Court's much awaited observation on live-in relationship on March 23, 2010 allows for a man and a woman in love, to live together and not a criminal offence, but the things are not as smooth as they seem to be. The concept is full of difficulties and hindrances.

How does the legal book of the country define live-in relationship?

The book of law in the country defines live-in relationship as a mutual understanding between two persons of different or same sex to live together. Hence, they can share the same house and get involved in all kinds of activities, just like a married couple, but, with each other's consent. Legally, they have no liabilities against each other, nor do they get any legal rights that they can enforce against each other which only a married couple have. Advocate B.T. Venkatesh said, "There is nothing wrong in a live-in relationship as long as it's of mutual understanding. Once, a couple decides to live-in together, there is no court of law, which can term it as a punishable offence. Whether one likes it or not, they have all the right to live under the same roof, provided, both the partners agree to it."

He explains, "A man and woman can live for as many years as they want, but no court of law will call it a crime. It's completely an individual's choice on what he wants; the relationship may end up with a marriage, or not, but the man is not entitled to any kind of punishment, so isn't the girl."

Following the courts order, many critics have argued that the Supreme Court's order favours man, and not the fairer sex. For instance, what if the couple have a child during the live-in relationship, and they decide to stay apart later in their life? "According to law, any child who is below 13 years of age will be under her mother's custody, unless for special reasons, like the mother could not be fit, mentally, to bring up the child. There are certain things like that, will be considered for that," said the advocate. Asserting his views on palimony, he explains, "Till the time a man and woman are not married, they don't get any privileges of a married couple, but, there is something called palimony."

But are there no laws at all that talk about a live-in relationship? "If only it can be proved, that it is a nature of marriage, which falls under domestic relationship. If the woman has a proof that the couple has been indulged in a domestic relationship, then the law comes into place. There are special considerations under domestic violence, which can be filed against the man, if he is involved in some kind of violent acts with his partner during their relationship."

The recent changes in the law against domestic violence promise equal benefits to women who are in live-in relationships. In simple terms, this means live-ins now get official stamp of recognition and women live-in partners get legal rights - just like wives. How much this judgement will save women or if they really need safety is a main question. Is it going to make any difference or it is going become another tool in the hands of cunning women to exploit their men folk?

National Commission of Women (NCW) recently proposed an amendment of Section 125 Criminal Procedure Code to include women involved in live-in relationships to be eligible for alimony from their live-in partners. This proposed amendment has far reaching consequences, which it is evident that the champion of women's causes, National Commission of Women seemed to have conveniently ignored.

Granting women, involved in live-in relationships a right to claim alimony is a direct insult of the most sacrosanct social institution, marriage, as in India, a marriage is a solemnised vow to support each other through all oddities, taken in the presence of community elders and with their blessings, but, in contrast, a live-in relationship is initiated by the couple just as a means to stay together. But unlike marriage, the commitment factor in a live-in relationship is very low as the ties are very easy to break. There are no liabilities involved from either side.

But giving women an extra and added advantage over men in a live-in relationship is illogical and out of rational to generalise and to assume that all relationships end due to men's fault and hence they should be made to pay for the same in the form of alimony. After totally lopsided and stringent provisions under the anti dowry provision, which have heavily been misused as per National Crime Records Bureau (NCRB) data, which has killed the institution of marriage silently; it seems it is now the turn of live-in relationships.

The law has been made on the generalised understanding that all men are criminals and all women are truthfully innocent. When there is a provision to extract money legally, why will a woman not initiate a live-in relationship, break it at will and then harass the man for whole life. As it is the concept of live-in relationship has not come of its age in the Indian society and will also not come as Indian societal scenario is hundred times more complex than Western society which is being beautifully attempted to be aped here.

And from here we see next step would be to legalise children born out of such relationships and such children will have deep psychological scars rendering them very vulnerable. Court is doing worst than ever! Rather than inviting women to start relationships and end them to earn tax-free money without doing any work, the NCW needs to condemn the very idea of live-in relationships and women should not get any sops so that they are discouraged to refrain from entering the wed ock.

As has been said earlier, there are apprehensions of the law being misused and abused by some women. It is quite logical that when the woman knows that she will get money only on levelling allegations, she cannot be expected to sacrifice and compromise to make the relation work. Such a provision can never ensure long lasting relationships.

Any relationship sustains on mutual understanding and enacting these and similar laws are going to add just some sourness. The wonderful relationship of husband and wife is going to be substituted with live-in relationship. Whatever would be the outcome of law this living relationship will harm women only in long term. Women may be flying high with their commercial success and high moral of newly earned liberty; in long run live-in relationship is return of feudalism and feudal values.

Illegitimate children not entitled to ancestral property: Supreme Court of India

The Supreme Court has ruled that children born out of a live-in relationship cannot inherit ancestral property, but only the self-acquired property of their parents.

"A child born of void or voidable marriage is not entitled to claim inheritance in ancestral coparcenary (joint inheritance) property but is entitled only to claim share in self-acquired properties, if any," the Apex Court said in an order.

A bench comprising Justice B S Chauhan and Swatanter Kumar passed the order while quashing a Madras High Court judgement which took the view that children born out of live-in relationships were entitled to a share in ancestral property.

In the instant case, a dispute arose whether the two children of Rengammal born on account of a live-in relationship with a bachelor Muthu Reddiar were entitled to a share in the latter's ancestral property after his death.

"In the instant case, respondents (claimants) had not pleaded at any stage that the suit land was a self-acquired property of Muthu Reddiar," the Apex Court said.

"It is evident from the record that Muthu Reddiar did not partition his joint family properties and died issueless / intestate in 1974. Therefore, the question of inheritance of coparcenary property by the illegitimate children, who were born out of the live-in relationship, could not arise," it said.

Muthu's relatives had contended that Rengammal was already married to one Alagarswami Reddiar and hence the purported live-in relationship was void and neither she nor her children can stake claim for a share in the property.

A civil court and the first appellate court both ruled in favour of Muthu's relatives on the ground that Rengammal was already married to Alagarswami and hence her illegitimate children were not entitled to any share in ancestral property.

However, the High Court took the view that mere live-in relationship between two parties would lead to presumption of marriage and decided the case in favour of Rengammal.

Interpreting the Hindu Marriage Act, the Apex Court said that Section 16 recognised the right of a child to inherit properties of their illegitimate parents, provided it was self-acquired. In view of the legal fiction contained in section 16, the illegitimate children for all practical purposes, including succession to the properties of their parents, have to be treated as legitimate.

"They cannot, however, succeed to the properties of any other relation on the basis of this rule, which in its operation is limited to the properties of the parents," the Apex Court said citing an earlier judgement in the PEK Kalliana Amma (1976) case.

10

Views After the Final Verdict

A girl is an IT professional, who hails from West Bengal, works in an Multi National Company (MNC) and stays in Mumbai in a two-room flat with her boyfriend. They term their relation as a "cool relationship" - he picks up the bills for groceries and she picks up the bills for the hired help. While he cooks on the weekend, she cooks on the weekdays. At the same time, they have schedules, which are in perfect coherence. In this smooth relationship, there just seems to be one downside - neither of their parents knows about the arrangement.

What has stopped them from disclosing their live-in status? Are they not confident about their relationship or do they feel they are doing something wrong? She says, "Neither do I feel that I am doing wrong and nor do I feel that my relationship cannot be disclosed as it will not last. I am perfectly confident about my relationship and my parents already know that he is the guy that I would eventually marry. They are also aware that we meet regularly or in most cases share meals - however, they do not know is that he has permanently moved in with me. I have consciously not told them about this decision. I feel that though they will not object but they will not understand either."

For him, moving in with his girlfriend seemed to be the best option as both of them "wanted to be together forever, and given their hectic schedules they hardly got any time to meet." So, this was the only option left open for them, he says. However, he, who hails from Madhya Pradesh, has not told his parents for a similar reason. "They are very traditional and cannot digest it," he rues.

Another couple, who are a live-in couple staying in Bangalore, have, however, told their family about their live-in status. "Initially, they were upset but now they have taken it in their stride, as they know that eventually we will get married. However, they have strictly asked us not to make this knowledge public," says the girl.

With the Supreme Court passing a judgment recently legalising live-in relationship and pre-marital sex, has their position improved? She answers in negative. "There was never any question of legality or morality for me; I am a consenting adult and I know what I am doing when I am living with somebody. So, the Supreme Court judgment does not really affect me at all, as I have no qualms about what I am doing; but maybe, it is a good initiative as all people are not like me and I hope this judgment can change their mind," she says.

Advocate Soumyajit Raha, however, feels that there are a lot of questions that the law does not answer. "What happens when a guy breaks up a relationship after five years of living together? In many cases, in such situations the girl brings charges under Sections 420 and 376. However, in such a situation, would it be justified, if the girl had been consenting partner in the relationship? Similarly, would it be justified if a partner walks out after years simply because the couple has been in a live-in relationship and not marriage? There needs to be a lot of introspection on these laws as after the aim of the law should be to safeguard the social well-being of a nation's citizens."

While advocate Raha feels that there should be more stringent regulations to define these laws, social worker Namita Sinha feels that if stringent rules are imposed, then the spirit of live-in relationship would be lost. "If there are strict rules associated with a live-in relationship, then what would be the point in having such a relationship and not going for marriage? There would be no difference left between the two," she adds.

Psychologist Anamika Ghoshe, who works with an NGO, however, feels that these two forms of relationship are essentially not different at all. "In fact, the emotional investment in both kinds of relationship is often the same. It would be wrong to say that a person is less disturbed when a live-in relationship breaks than when a marriage breaks; so, psychologically there is no significant difference between the two."

Ghoshe feels that despite sex being a taboo word in tradition-bound societies like India, young people today are more open to the concept of pre-marital sex and live-in relationship. "In fact, most young people today are keen on checking their physical compatibility with their partners before they opt for long-term relationships; so, they are open to the idea of a live-in relationship and concept of pre-marital sex as well. What they do not want is the unnecessary chastisement by society, and for this they often practice the same behind closed doors while keeping the society guessing," she adds.

Are most of the senior Indians against the concept of live-in or pre-marital sex? An elderly homemaker, who has been married for more than 30 years, says: "To be frank, yes. At least, in my case I would not be happy if my daughter, who is a graduate and who works as a designer, enters a live-in relationship. I would always want her to be traditionally married as I am and would feel insecure for her if she stays in a live-in relationship. However, on retrospection I think, I would adjust - after all if she stays with a partner of opposite sex despite him being of different caste/community, I would think that all would finally turn out to be well." Like her, another woman, a mother of two teenaged daughters, feels that "live-in is fine if it finally leads to marriage." She is open to "free mixing" of her daughters but would want them to be "finally married and settled in future."

Given the changing times, it seems an increasing number of people are embracing the liberal way of living and loving. The Supreme Court judgment, which states, "Living together is not an offence" clearly reflects this changed scenario. Advocate Raha points out that the apex court's judgment is reflective of a changed social scenario. "Prevalence of live-in relationship is on rise and the Supreme Court's judgment is reflective of this changing social trend.

"A recent judgment of the court has also extended the law on domestic violence to cover live-in relationships - in fact, as live-in relationship becomes an imminent reality more thought needs to be given to safeguard the interests and rights of people in such relationships. At the same time, a clear line needs to be drawn between marriage and live-in relationship. It should be ensured that in a bid to give rights to live-in relationships, the institution of marriage is not threatened," Raha says.

With the legalised status being given to live-in relationship a major question that arises is whether the "legalised" live-in partner is considered equal to the wife / husband, if one of the partners happens to be married. Advocate Raha feels that this would not be true and despite legalisation of live-in relationship, a live-in partner would not have the right of a married partner. "The laws of adultery and bigamy still hold true - after all, they are prevalent laws and any new law cannot conflict with an existing law. One person's / woman's right cannot jeopardise another woman's happiness," he says.

Despite all these controversies, it seems this verdict on live-in relationship has had a positive impact on the youngsters. "The law shows that times are changing and people are accepting the changed social norms. In a few years down the line, I believe, it would change further and common people, too, will agree that there is nothing moral / immoral about a live-in relationship," says a girl who is living-in.

Her partner, however, feels that it will take a long time to come. "As long as the end relationship is marriage, it would be tough for people to acknowledge openly that they are in a live-in relationship - after all, there is something eternally fairy tale and romantic about marriage. Staying in a live-in relationship somehow, spoils that and I think this is a major reason why people are reluctant to accept," he smiles as he speaks. For most of these youngsters in a live-in relationship, this relationship seems to be a matter of convenience and a means of testing water before they plunge into the "stable" marriage relationship.

Sociologist Oindrila Mitra says, "This, however, will not be an easy task. Sex has forever been taboo in our society and the concept of pre-marital sex is something that is not acceptable. Even today, for most people, a live-in relationship is a vile concept that defies the sanctity of marriage. Most couples, who live together, hope to get married someday. Given this scenario, it would be difficult to change the mindset of people as far as living together or pre-marital sex is concerned. A law cannot change the attitude of society.

For most people, a live-in relationship continues to be a vile concept that defies the sanctity of marriage. Even many of the couples, who live together, hope to get married someday." she says.

Sowmya, Kannur, Kerala - In recent years there has been a remarkable increase in the number of people opting for living-in relationships instead of marriages. Though this trend has been popular in Western countries for a long time now, it is catching up in India as well with more and more couples choosing to live-in, because of the space, choice and personal freedom it gives them. It might be immensely appealing to young people of today, leading hectic and stressful lives and do not have the time or patience to deal with all the emotional issues that a marriage entails. Apart from the space it gives, there is no problem of surrendering rights or obligations in a live-in relationship. The partners are pretty clear about what they are in for, and if the relationship does not work out, they can leave anytime. There are no legal or a financial complication involved, unlike a marriage, where splitting up is not so easy. But even in a live-in relationship, the situation becomes more complex if children are involved. Since, there is no binding relationship between the partners the issue of taking up responsibility for bringing up the children gets more complicated. Since there is no emotional security offered, it becomes difficult to sustain a long term relationship and there is a high risk of breaking up. The moment couples hit a rough patch, they find it easier to split than make efforts to make the relationship work.

Though marriages also have their pros and cons, no relationship enjoys the social and legal recognition as a marriage does. The obvious merits of a marriage are the emotional commitment and the support that the partners have for each other. Since a marriage is protected by law, couples expect loyalty and fidelity from each other. Further, marriage is an incentive to develop staying power in a relationship. There is a lot of emotional investment in the relationship. Though marriages also have their ups and downs with an increasing number of couples going for divorces in recent years, when it comes to commitment and security, no relationship can match a marriage. It is a bond that can last a lifetime.

One development that has caught everyone's attention in recent times has been the amendment to Section 125 of Criminal Procedure Code proposed by The National Commission for Women to include women involved in live-in relationships to be eligible for alimony from their live-in partners. Granting women involved in live-in relationships, a right to claim alimony is a serious insult of the most sacrosanct social institution, as in India, a marriage is a solemnised vow to support each other through thick and thin taken in the presence of community elders and with their blessings, but, in contrast, a live-in relationship is initiated by the couple just as a means to stay together. But unlike marriage, the commitment factor in a live-in relationship is very low as the ties are very easy to break and there are no liabilities involved from either side.

There is no denying that live-in relationships are proving to be extremely popular, particularly among educated urban classes, for whom living in is a declaration of independence, as a way of keeping away from the restrictions and inequalities of institutionalised marriages. But a live-in relationship can never replace marriage. It can never offer the kind of security and emotional fulfillment that a marriage does. "Marriage" is a word that makes some jittery and yet there are others who still believe in the sanctity of such a union and respect it. It's been a few years since the concept of "live-in" got introduced to our society and even though the Supreme Court may have granted the relationship all legalities equivalent to that of a marriage, our society may still not be ready to welcome it with open arms.

It is hard to deny the fact that in a country like ours, family plays a huge role and marriage seemingly is the stepping stone or rather the foundation of nurturing this concept. The reason why marriage has been and still is to a certain extent, a popular institution is because it provides an individual with companionship, security and stability in life. Marriage, as argued lends a sense of responsibility in life. But the traditional arguments and beliefs have not been able to restrain the current fast paced generation from finding a convenient solution. 'Live-in!' a concept initially viewed as one of the adverse effects of Westernisation has now carved a niche in some strata of the society. It is no more a mere rebellious statement made by young adults but a mature decision. Some people feel that there is no harm in a live-in relationship if it is a prelude to marriage, as it helps one to know the better half better. Though such a relationship or an arrangement has always been under the ethical radar and vigil of moral police, these days it is just a matter of saving money. For many, live-in relationship is the preference because it is time to change and evolve with the changing times, though it might seem socially incorrect.

It might offer one space, help us understand our companion more but at the end of the day, many who are not against the idea of live-in still feel marriage is their first or rather only preference. Even though such practices are not alien to our history and our present, the fact remains, that as a society for the general middle class population, living without a customary authorisation isn't and wouldn't be acceptable for a long time to come. So marriage is a must. Besides there is also the opinion that someone who opts for a live-in might get bored or satisfied and leave for no concrete reason. However in case of a marriage people at least try to work it out.

The pros and cons of both arrangements have always been before us. For those who believe live-in is a cultural violation, it would never gain respect and for those who are moving with the times, it is the perfect arrangement. Either ways the choice is ours. Like it's said, "Nothing is right or wrong: Thinking makes it so", if you feel you can't handle the responsibility, the apparent monotonous tone of married life and you need space, freedom, live-in is the answer. In the end, whatever relationship one chooses, it should be an arrangement where interests of both the partners are kept in mind and there is an understanding and commitment between the two. It is just a matter of perception; one can take a marriage as a live-in arrangement or have a live-in like marriage.

Bakshinder (excerpts from articlebase) - The recent remarks of the Supreme Court of India, on live-in relationships and pre-marriage sex, have raised many eyebrows. However, greater analysis of the subject made me realise that the apex legal body has changed with the times. We keep criticising one and all on such issues. But, a deeper thought would change your opinion and outlook on this.

Relationship mathematically is a subset of sex. Both have to co-exist and follow one another to complete the activity of sacred union. Nothing is good or bad in this universe if one is fully convinced of being right. It is only one's conviction that is of essence in this. Why did people get married earlier? What was the objective of doing so? One may say that like the revolution in communication of earlier times of writing a letter and the present instant 'SMSing' services, there is a revolution in relationship. Objectives are the same but the activity has been fast forwarded.

However, like the fundamental rights there are fundamental duties. One just cannot justify rights forgetting the duties. This new change should be taken in a more positive and responsible way. The live-in relationship and sex before marriage is a serious activity that should be indulged in with all seriousness and sincerity. If you misuse it, it will misuse you both. It is a really private affair and need not be discussed in public.

Finally, the concepts of live-in relationship and pre-marriage sex have now started gaining the recognition of statutory bodies. Everyone is changing with the time which is a welcome sign. However, if one indulges in it just for fun or time pass activity, it will result in an explosion of dynamite which is in immature hands. The result will be negative for people involved in particular and society in general. So, think over it before convincing yourself or your mate that Supreme Court has given you a license to go for the kill.

Agreed

The neo intellectuals in the society keep different views on the issue of live-in relationship. They call all those opposing live-in relationship as 'Custodians of Public Morality'. While advocating freedom for choosing a live-in relationship they emphasize an individual's right to decide for self. They strongly oppose conventional, orthodox thinking denying them freedom to live life on their own terms.

They do not approve age old puritan thinking. Why should others decide what is good and what is bad for them, they argue? It's their life after all and they have the right to live it the way they want to. If they are comfortable with live-in relationship why should they enter into a marital contract? Western influence is quite discernable in their approach to the Social issues.

Chandler Perez, Nebraska, U.S.A. - In Society marriage became an institution, with two specific purposes.

1. To ensure the paternity of a child is certain. As they used to say, maternity is a fact, and Paternity is a matter of opinion.

But that's no longer true. Paternity can be accurately identified.

2. It was an implicit (sacred) contract that bound two people for life.

The society needed a method to enforce a discipline where a couple will stick through thick and thin. The idea was to provide for a mechanism which put a moral pressure on the couple to stay together. But, this necessity started breaking down when society started permitting the divorce (an accepted way of dissolving a contract). With the result, many people considered marriage to be the only permissible way to have sex. This was natural in days of non-availability of Birth control, as if people engaged in casual sex, then paternity couldn't be decided.

This not being the case, and marriages susceptible to dissolution, the institution of marriage is indeed purely one of choice, rather than a social necessity. So, it is but natural that legal system will support live-in and casual sex.

Whenever any progressive event takes place, the Indians always start talking of Indian culture to discourage that event. I have studied Indian culture and going by that, they should be burning their widows and marrying off their kids too. That's not the point; they must take what's relevant and discard what is not.

How can live-in relationships become a menace? How does it bother you if two people are consenting to live together or have sex? It is between them. As Supreme Court of India has rightly asked - What law are they breaking? This is just a step for free sex. I'd say three cheers. It is right to life, because sex is part of life.

If a foreigner has a live-in relation then what will be citizenship of the child. If a child is born in a country, he is natural citizen of that country. What is the ambiguity here?

But, it indeed is strange that the Supreme Court should invoke religious references to a question that is purely in the domain of Logic and Law. Of course, not because of mythology, but the jury were just asking a rhetorical question to people who pointed to the Indian culture as reason against live-in relationships.

Jurisprudence normally works on the basis of 'locus standi', which means, you must be directly impacted by an event to be a party to a court case. Even in case of a Public Interest Litigation, in India, the people filing case should be able to show themselves, as part of public, being affected.

The argument of the people complaining about the actor Kushboo's statement was that acceptance of pre-marital sex will lead to relaxation of social pressures for the girls to stay virgin until marriage Why the folks aren't worried about the boys. So, the Indian Apex Court was questioning their locus standi in the matter.

The first and foremost purpose of marriage which (I suppose) gave birth to the inception of this institution was largely to make the determination about paternity of a child easy. In fact, till few years back, men were allowed multiple marriages (even Non-Muslims), but women not being allowed to do so is based on this basic fact - Paternity wasn't easy to decide, but Maternity was. Today with Paternity tests, that requirement is no longer true.

But the second purpose of marriage still remains good. For many it is a sacred contract with another person with a mutual obligation to respect, love and be there for duration of the contract, ideally life long - with or without children in the picture.

Anarchy means lawlessness. Gays, Pre-marital sex etc. doesn't break the law, as derived from constitution, as defined by Supreme Court of the land. Thus – 'No Anarchy'! Anarchy happens when our system allows motivated people to browbeat people who don't agree with them – Ram Senes, Bajarang Dal etc.(hardcore Hindu groups) etc.

We need to protect and promote 'Marriage', 'Family' and 'Family Values'. It is an institution to cherish and needs to be promoted.

But, this can't be done thru law, which derives its legitimacy from a libertine constitution to let people follow their own faith. Who is to say 'Not marrying can't be an article of faith to someone' and who is to say 'just because a person wants to have sex with someone, he needs to enter into a lifelong, binding contract'?

A hundred years back West's system was more like that of India, Victorian morality, marriages lasting lifelong etc. Today's Western value system is based on Individual liberties with social security being ensured by their respective Governments. Today's Western world doesn't understand much about 'arranged marriages' and also people sticking to marriage.

Indian value system is based on the old Victorian system. They probably will move the same direction West did, over next 100 years (if world survives) or so... Divorce rates will increase; pre-marital sex will be the norm. Institution of Arranged Marriages will start fading away – with individual rights becoming supreme - thus people being able to rely on a different kind of social security. Each generation changes the society (for better or worse). I am not saying what is happening is good or bad. It is too early to tell. But, it will definitely happen.

Marriage and monogamy may not serve a purpose in future, because paternity can be determined and security of progeny can be ensured through other legal means. Procreation instincts can be satisfied through sex without children.

The bottom-line for folks who don't like liberty of others to do things within the framework of law is – 'GROW UP'.

Liju Philip, Mumbai, India - Because the parents never had the chance, they object to their kids' enjoyment.

Because people speaking of religious and cultural reasons are morons who love discriminating against people based on religion, caste, creed, colour etc.

I think the whole spectrums of people who object have been covered.

Why can't the society just stop criticising every new thing and leave to the choice of the people in general....? What in the world is the harm in staying together with a person with whom you can relate and spend quality time... and being 'sensible' at the same time. For those who call it to be against 'the Indian culture' should remember that we have already come a long way and things which are apparently not our culture's part are quite prevalent.

Ranu, Vishakhapatnam, India - This relation which is being adopted in our society shows that society is also progressive and by and by it is getting modern in veritable manner. Though who try to promote cultural value in the name of tradition are facing threat of social modernism, that's why they are insecure.

Two individuals want to live together before tying knot with each other! Fine! WHAT IS WRONG IN THAT? These individuals have every right to try out each other before getting into a long lasting relationship! And why not!

Times have changed now! Therefore, the societal viewpoint that live-in relationships and pre-marital sex will lead to society degeneration is absolute non-sense. Over the centuries, the law and society has defined the age when an individual becomes a major and is permitted to take decisions related to his physical and emotional needs. The right to do so - after he becomes an adult - goes much beyond the constitutional right; it is his / her birth right.

This is '**NOT**' to challenge the institution of marriage, which has its own sanctity and has been established and practiced by mankind for long. The point of contention is that grown up adults, past legal age of being called adults, have a choice to decide whether and when to get married and that right cannot be taken away by fringes of society which have nothing better to do but to enforce their right to interfere in the personal matters of adults by intimidation. The Supreme Court, through its comments, aims to confirm the rights of the former.

The changed world has meant higher education for both sexes with plenty of employment opportunities coming their way. There are more nuclear families than ever before. Men and women live away from families for studies and then for work. They are more independent! Couples need to balance out career, money matters and plan a child responsibly. They need to figure out the right time for marriage. Women are especially empowered and aware of their rights. Today's couple is more knowledgeable of their physical and emotional wellbeing and its importance in their happiness. There is no harm if they wish to try each other out (physically and emotionally) before committing to marriage and as Supreme Court comments; they have this right under constitution.

One cannot go wrong when it comes to judging each other's partners' nature, living habits and other facets before marrying each other, as later they don't have to blame anyone, if their relationship faces hurdles in future!

Vidyacharan Shukla, Nanded - Indian culture is changing dramatically but in different colors. Intrinsically, we are plagued with double standards that manifest time to time in the form of litigation, complaints and blames just to hide our own lusts. Pre-marital relationship has prevailed everywhere around the globe but Indian society preferred to suppress the facts, instead of facing the truth.

Philosophically, even we dream about the physical relationship before marriage or after marriage, both are considered to be sin if we follow any religion. No religion stops anyone living together and law of nature supports Khusboo's bold stand. It is sad that Supreme Court has to intervene in this case but giving decision in the favour of Khusboo shows the faith on the judiciary. Supreme Court's judges' cited beautiful example of Lord Krishna and Goddess Radha, but the better examples could have been of Kanyakumari with Lord Shiva and many more who are our Ideals in Indian society.

Cinthia Alex, Goa - It's an individual's choice whether to get into a live-in relationship or not.... Nobody is forcing you... and people should not talk about Indian culture all the time. There are many things which we follow which aren't parts of Indian culture... and anyway the word must not be 'legalising' but official recognition..... It's already legal and it comes under the freedom of choice....

There are many brave hearts who marry for sex and dowry and have little hesitation in killing the bride. Marriage is also a legalised sex which comes free, dominated by male, while live together has little exception. At least the sense of guilt will go and the togetherness will grow in a healthy atmosphere and the ladies will be able to express themselves free from fear, domination and humiliation. This will be a mature marriage of consent instead of first night rape by an unknown, sex hungry stranger absolutely lacking in knowledge of sex and devoid of any emotion and love. This is worse than prostitution where two people have prior consent of sex without any expectation except money. This is an unending debate. I welcome the step which may free our mind from guilt and dogmas.

I think it's a good move. It's a good step towards broadening our mindsets and will help accept the changes with the changing times and adapt them and not take it in a negative way. At least now illegitimate children would not suffer the label of being called "********" for no fault of their own. Institution of marriage is a very sacred thing and people will stop getting married. At least now people will marry only if they want to and not just to legalise their relationship. Now, the institution of marriage will be much more august than ever as this will be the outcome of long companionship and knowledge of each other for a graceful mutual acceptance.

Srini Ahlawat, Chandigarh, India - Hats off to Kushboo and appreciate the bold announcement of judges. Let's see a mature India in the future.

There is nothing wrong in the live-in relationships. What's the big deal in that? If two persons are willing to do so, let them do so. I think nowadays people are smart and mature enough to know what's right for them and they can take their own decisions.

Living together without marriage is a human right and it should not be mixed with culture. The strains of marriage should not deny a person the enjoyment of sex.

Great decision by the Supreme Court! Self-appointed moral police have no business in dictating the private lives of individuals. What the judges had meted out should enlighten parents as to understand that their daughters and sons need sexual pleasure with respect and it is not by sale.

Shridhar Sadasivan, Hyderabad - Just because you don't agree with the other person's point of view (in this case, Kushboo's), it doesn't make them criminals. What Supreme Court said is not against culture. It is called freedom of speech. It is actually in favour of good culture that we Indians had before sexism, caste system and hypocrisy had crept in.

Hats off to Kushboo! It takes lot of courage and determination to stand up against bigotry and prejudice. And living together is far better than the so called 'arranged marriages' which lead to loveless marriage, marital rape, wife abuse, domestic violence, suppression of women etc. etc.

Thou it is unfortunate that such matter had to go to court but it is great to see the outcome! We all must applaud the Supreme Court for its stand in this matter. There has to be a clear distinction between a set of moral values, and the law of the land. "Living together" was once known as "living in sin", but since those days, the world has changed a great deal. The question here is not as much about whether it is right or wrong - but whether we as a society can dictate the private lives of our citizens.

The Supreme Court has been very right in questioning if the law is broken when two consenting adults decide to live together. As long as there is no violation of the law, it should not be anyone's concern.

Simon Timothy, Pune, India - Can this judgement be used against the self-made moral polices like MNS, Bajrang Dal (political parties in India) and other such parties that made news in Mangalore and Bangalore recently? Why the State Governments are soft against such groups? Why not take action against them immediately? It feels very good to know that in spite of the bias about women and the rampant moral policing in the name of god, religion, moral values etc., there still are a bunch of able, sensible and wise judges running the highest court of law in our country.

This is a Great Decision. Hats off to the Supreme Court and hope the moral policemen, parties, politicians, and organisations of our nation keep their mouth Shut once and for all. Finally it looks like India is marching towards a matured democracy. Highly appreciate this bold judgement and comments.

Rajasekaran Elangovan, Singapore - The very fact that our Judiciary is taking 5 years to deliver justice in 2010 for a speech made in 2005 is highly disheartening though. This is a fantastic decision by the Supreme Court of India, which continues to be an epitome of prudence and perspicacity. Is it not a fundamental right of the citizens to live as they choose to? Being offended by others' views and actions at the drop of a hat seems to have become a norm.

We are compelled to question why the Madras High Court dismissed Khushboo's plea to dismiss the criminal proceedings against her in the lower courts. At last, a good blow to self-proclaimed moral police brigades. Now the hypocrites should be silenced until another progressive person is made a scapegoat. Until then, long lives the freedom of speech in India!

D. Chandorkar, Aurangabad, Maharashtra - A certainly landmark judgement made by the Apex Court. A judgement that makes sense in a country where all types of nonsense goes around in the name of culture. Our democracy is awesome and the Supreme Court Judges are powerful in their judgement. I salute the Jury.

The Supreme Court has taken a legalistic view in disposing of the case, and rightly so. India will escape from bottom of the list of countries based on Human Development Index only when people and society at large do not poke their nose in the life of individuals. However, the time-tested societal laws concerning marriages and family relationships need to be honoured. So, it would be welcomed if celebrities who are endowed with the power to influence masses could avoid expressing drastic views.

However, infringing one's right to express opinion is to be upheld. Harassing them, in whatever way, should be condemned. What a man and woman, who are adults, do in the privacy of their room and which does not physically injure another person is no business of the society or the rest of the people.

Luhar Sen, Durgapur, West Bengal - Good judgement by the Supreme Court! Well the Supreme Court has encouraged democracy! People have criticised it by saying that it will bring fall of our country (society). Living together is a human right and these things or anyone's personal opinion should not be mixed with one's morality or our culture.

If by this legendary decision as far as falling of India goes then let me ask caste system, dowry and honour killings go unabated in our country. Aren't these things leading to a fall of our country? If not then how can an individual's choice to live according to them will lead to a fall of our country! This ruling should have come many years earlier. Better late than never!

On the one side, we in India, have a semi-literate society that does not hesitate to glorify violence, impossible romance and sex in movies, and on the other side, rigid social structures and a bunch of people who act as moral police and think it is in their prerogative to check people's personal lives. The result is a frustrated, stunted, and sexually immature society.

Not to forget that India has one of the highest numbers of HIV infected people. The so-called champions of Indian culture do not however for once, pause to question 'WHY' all this is taking place. Of course, it is ever so easy to transfer the blame onto the West, which the moral police think it can interpret without even setting its foot there. Better than trying to stifle and suppress natural feelings, and impose unscientific standards, would be to offer a transparent healthy sex education to youngsters, informing them of their rights, and making them more aware of sexual matters, safety etc. Indian culture has a lot to gain by cultivating a well-informed society of mature and healthy people, which can enjoy normal human freedom, and making them more critically aware of the social contexts they live in, rather than producing dead and numb conformists for who even the freedom of speech is a crime. It is also pertinent to ask why rapes, molestations, and other crimes against women are commonplace in India.

The judgement by the Supreme Court of India is fully justified.

Brijesh Mishra, Hardoi, India - Everything on earth is changeable. Nothing remains like yesterday. Everything has changed in the past about 20 years in India but why are we continuing with lifetime risky old marriage system. This might be good in the past but in a fast changing scenario how can we continue with the age old system whereas we have changed almost every system? Particularly it should be seen in context with endless sex crimes, increasing dangerous HIV cases, falling male/female ratio. And to add to the problems girls are not willing to marry these days. One does not marry to take divorce or to go for live-in relationship in future but what will happen when one day he or she finds that things are not good and working as expected and life is going hell? Almost 80 percent of the married couples are unhappy and pulling their lives unpleasantly! Live-in relationship will be a sigh of relief to start their life again.

There are already so many rules to help females in India and misused by them but is there any rule to help males? Just to please your 50 percent vote bank of female voters you don't want a good and healthy solution? How one can live with somebody whom he or she does not like at all? If you make an opinion poll of married couples whether they want to change their partners then perhaps 80 percent (both male / female) will opt for change.

The difficult part about this entire scenario is that our country requires intervention of Supreme Court to decide on key human relations areas as well. However, this judgement has brought a new hope in the hopelessness of married life for both men and women. There is nothing wrong in trying out you're would be spouse before tying the knot. I salute the judges for their far sightedness and excellent judgement.

I hope all the local cops are updated about the news. If not, firstly they must be made aware about the judgement because they are the one who still try to disturb young couples who want to have a live-in relationship.

Aakanksha Bhanot, Amritsar, Punjab - India is a strange mix of tradition and modernity and as it stands a very confused society. We also have understood that we are multi religion society and approval of government agencies and that of political spectrum will also keep this into consideration. My take is that such situations will happen in metropolitan cities. Couples have been maintaining live-in (which includes pre-marital sex) relationships, especially in metros, and they do not really bother what others have to say regarding this. Supreme Court has come up with its comment bit late, however, now we can at least expect small town people to be liberal with the concept... In the end love should conquer. Sex, live-in, marriage - they are all status. A living-in couple can be happier than one married and vice versa. It differs in all individual situations.

Sachin Shroff, Faridabad, Haryana - We disapprove of pre-marital sex for women because women need to be as pure as possible. Let's face it, all the responsibility of keeping the moral fiber of the society together is with the woman, isn't it? So there, no pre-marital sex for women and the objective of sex is only to have progeny!

But seriously, this two-facedness of our society is remarkable. On one hand we are all right with little girls who are married and being underage mothers, but we are not fine with our adult single women living in with their boyfriends and doing what couples do.

As humans we are so hung up on sex. Consider this. 'Not only it is "wrong" to live-in (because if you probably have sex outside of marriage, its wrong, perform a simple ceremony and have sex, voila, it stops being "dirty"), it is also the "greatest sin" someone can commit.'

We actually believe morality is something that dangles between our legs

I think moral policing is about being more in the other person's bedroom than really caring for crime and such, because it is in societies that are most heavily morally policed that the greatest crimes against women occur.

Look at India for instance. We do not have sex education

in school - it is so against our culture, yet about one third children are molested in this country (there was a BBC report on this). And let's not even talk about the amount of crimes against women (carefully trivialised as eve teasing) that occur.

In India victims of sexual crimes are generally made to feel like they invited the crime by being at the wrong time, with a wrong person, wearing the wrong clothes at the wrong place... and then of course the biggest worry is the dishonour which they bring (not the rapist or the molester) to their family.

Do you know in many places in India, the mother-in-law sleeps next to a woman who has just delivered, to make sure her husband doesn't force himself on her? So let's try not to compare us to women in the West. The difference is women in the West can walk out of a relationship or complain about a rapist if they choose to, an average Indian woman can't.

Indian women are always being reminded how lucky they are to be born in India, where they are worshiped as Goddesses, unlike the bad West – 'the land of teen pregnancies' where women are exploited.

Joe Mullen, Hong Kong – Live-in doesn't have any age limit. If you feel you wanna do it just do it...just spend time with your loved ones while the feel is not yet gone! I think its fine; I have been living with my love since I was 18, and now I am 21. My girlfriend and I are putting up in two different residences because our parents are paying the rent for them, but we spend every night with each other. College is the one aspect parents have no control over it.

Abeer Mukopadhyay, Suffolk, U.K. – "Man loves a woman to get sex whereas a woman offers sex to get love" is a famous and a vastly accepted saying. Thus India's Supreme Court's judgement is certainly going to axe the infidelity of men. One should analyse without any bias the judgements made by the Honourable Supreme Court before jumping to any conclusion.

Religious reasons, societal tension, and fear of getting pregnant usually forced many to abstain from sex until marriage. However, in reality, physical intimacy before marriage is widely practiced in India, both in metropolitan cities and small towns.

A recent study conducted by the Population Council found that 17 percent men in rural areas are engaged in pre-nuptial sex compared to 10 percent in cities, while 4 percent women in rural areas engaged in sex before marriage against 2 percent in cities.

The whole thing is that it's prevalent in our society and culture is something which goes on with time, changes and takes its shape. One just can't hold this back in the name of religion, values and morality. Youths in India are very much aware about morality, career and family. After all, what's wrong when there is stability with no disorder?

Laxman Vernekar, Kerala, India - You don't need marriage to breed. Once education levels increase in India, there should be a drop in birth rates. Even in India, educated people who are settled tend to have lesser children than those who are not - married or not.

You promote whatever you want, Khushboo has the same right as you do - as long as both of you are not breaking any law of the land. Let the Supreme Court worry about the constitution, denial of basic rights and social justice (to majority of people) and the backlog that clogs the system. We can move on to metaphysical discussions and religious debate when we are ready.

I am for live-in relationship and all for legalising live-in relationships, especially since this will secure the couple from some potential idiot-allegations of prostitution. If the couple is sure that they are going to be together long-term, it's often advantageous to get a registered marriage certificate (helps during travel, immigration, visas etc.) but if they never plan on leaving their home town they can save on the registration costs. One thing I'd like to see happen in India is the concept of prenuptial agreements. It'd protect men from potential gold digger women.

Why the urge to have exclusive sexual access in men? The basic instinct driving this feeling would be to ensure paternity right? After all by nature most men want to have exclusive sexual access to a woman, but on the other hand want to have sex with as many women as they can (which I guess we suppress with cultural conditioning / marriage law etc. which are a control mechanism to prevent anarchy for greater good of society).

Shehnaz Bootwala, India—It is disappointing to see so many comments which are almost one-sided. (Just like the moral brigade on the prowl). It's plain and simple – living-in and pre-marital sex are not illegal. Somebody had to pronounce it and the Supreme Court did that. Whilst there are people who are already doing the same, it must be noted that the Court isn't forcing people to do the same. It simply says it's not illegal. Well, I fail to understand why there is this talk about marriage being an institution, free sex etc. etc. If divorce can be legal then why not living-in and pre-marital sex? What is the harm when two consenting adults get to enjoy sex - This is what appears the Court said?

We need to think we have moved beyond that and are reasonably rational.

Teenage and pre-marital sex has caused massive problems in the West. How can teenagers having sex cause tremendous problems? It's just like recreation. So what if a child is born out of wedlock? Do they abandon or what? What do we mean by children not brought up properly? Do we think children are brought up very properly here?

India may be shining in bits and pieces and I would love to see this Race go forward.

Amaury Quentin, Amiens, France - I always hate to be married to a woman and making her wishes to submerge for my sake and then not allowing her to do her job correctly. It's not a fair means on this aspect and also that to restrict her ambitions to my own wishes. I will support those who think that just being friends in the life, will serve better than getting married.

It is true that live-in relationships are more preferred through out the world these days. But a live-in relationship is still a commitment. You have to share costs, household chores and most importantly space. You have to learn how to negotiate and that sometimes you can't have everything your own way. When I started living with my girlfriend, I considered it a commitment. We lived together for about 2 years, before we got married. It was just a natural process. At the time we couldn't afford to get married and we also needed to get to know each other a little more.

Nidhi Joglekar (excerpts from wordpress) - In case you are struggling morally, socially and individually to find the answer of the questions the Supreme Court has asked, the Bench has one for you. "Living together is not a sin. It is not illegal and cannot be defined as 'criminal offence'." The example of Radha and Krishna settles the religious, mythological questions of credibility!

Our legal torchbearers seem to be scoring good on the social reform chart, the glamour industry feels elated by the news (like it had any effect on them before); the moral police are aghast and the rebels impressed (for a change)! We try finding out the views of the common man, who still suffers from the decriminalisation of Article 377 (of the Indian Constitution) hangover, on the subject.

Arjun Kundu, an IT professional from Mohali, says "I feel it is another bold decision taken by the highest judiciary in the country. I think it should have been done 25 years back. The decision represents India as a freethinking society where stereotypes should be broken. Now, people will be guilt-free while making choices about their life."

Anupama Gupta (a teacher by profession) supports the judgement by saying, "Why is everybody so fixed up on this subject? It's a personal thing and should not affect the overall moral count of the country." And they have an advice for the moral police as well.

Gaurav feels, "Their focus should be to protest against rape, sexual harassment, eve-teasing and not on curtailing somebody's freedom. I think it is a positive move and one should not make a big deal out of it. If one has to walk out of a relationship, live-ins still is a better option than divorces."

Disagreed

On the other side those opposed to the idea of live-in relationship, question the relevance of the institution of marriage in the backdrop of permissiveness in the society. They lay emphasis on the Social and Moral values which have been followed in India for centuries. As per 'Dharam Shastra' (a Hindu Scripture), they say, the right to bear a child is only to a married couple. It can be exciting in the beginning to share a room with a friend or acquaintance of opposite sex but at the end of the day romance of the relationship disappears and the couple has to face stark reality of the practical world. Who bears the brunt of the consequences (kids)?

Pragati Sahay, a Human Resource professional, has objected to the judgement like many other people. "Other than the personal sustainability of a live-in relationship and the commitment hassles are involved, I believe it is not accepted because of the culture bend. It's like asking an Irani woman to go without Burqa in their homeland."

Ann Carlson, Germany – I have been studying the Indian Culture since long. India is among the best cultural nations of the world. Due to this other nations look towards India with respect. The virus of live-in relationship has entered into India. There is need to stop this virus, before it causes big damage. Once it becomes strong, then it will be so tough to throw it out. Unfortunately some people have started the implementation of live-in relationship. There are so many families in India which live together as joint family. We cannot compare the live-in relationship with this joint family relationship as maintaining relations for enjoying sex-life and for maintaining happy family life are totally different.

It means the lifestyle will change to use and throw condition. We know very well the situation in most of the countries where certain people aie free to indulge in sex in open. Such people become so mad about sex and think of nothing better by putting limitations in their lives and ultimately turning their life to untold miseries and at the end they commit suicide. In front of physical attractions they should not forget their parents who have so simple expectations from them. Try to understand the meaning of love; love is not only physical relations but understanding each other. Marriage maintains the cycle of society. What we will tell to next generation that living life means only live-in relationships?

The Supreme Court of India's recent ruling that "the right to live-in with a partner without certificate of marriage is a fundamental one: and that the pre-marital sex is not illegal - there being no prohibiting law", is only the legal statement - devoid of moral and social aspects. Such live-in relations are based on selfishness, having no place for sincerity and guarantee for a lasting relationship. Such relationship will exploit the weaker one and blackmail the immorality of abortion or MTP (Medical Termination of Pregnancy) and the unwanted bastards are inevitable curses.

In the West the people are disillusioned by truant sex and are returning to the sacred sanctuary of wedlock to seek blessings of the Church. We must realise that live-in relationship is *La Vida Loco*, polluting our society and ethics. These forbidden apples are like immoral, live-inns on life's highway, and must be nipped in the bud.

Ziauddin Shafi, Ajman, Emirates - It's nothing but a preview of how corrupted our values have become. Live-in relationship is simply a "Western" way of escaping from your responsibilities. Remember that our thoughts today will probably be actions tomorrow and they will have consequences the day after. Evil desires of today will be sinful actions tomorrow and could probably have irreversible impact on the society as a whole.

Before branding the West, let us look into our own history and how the people have had live-in relationships. West is taking a roundabout turn towards spirituality, and we are marching full on into the arms of a life filled with stress, loss and pain and all that is bound to follow the inevitable erosion of our values. Remember that there are millions of Westerners who have been committed to their spouses till death parted them. Just because we see a few having troubled married lives, we cannot say the institution of marriage has failed.

Legalising live-in relationships are the equivalent licenses for couples tasting each other's bodies before going on to fresh pastures and fresh bodies, if I may be permitted to put across the point rather crassly or crudely. Having relationships before marriage can make a boy or girl repeat it secretly with their 'ex' even several years after the marriage. How many abortions can a woman undergo, if she has to keep on changing relationships?

Marriages in India are not a contract for union of two bodies; rather it is unity of 'ATMA' (soul) in two bodies. This is not prostitution. This live-in relationship is not 'Indian Culture'. Marriage means it is a responsibility towards the family and society. If family is good, the society will be good. If society is good, the nation will be good. If the nation is good everybody will be happy.

Premier NGO 'Sanjeevani Maa Ghara', India - A crusader for women's rights, has launched a postcard campaign against the verdict urging both men and women to register their opposition to the verdict with the President of

India and seek a revision in the Supreme Court of its own decree.

"We hope the Government shall take proper steps to safeguard Indian women's rights and dignity and save the society from chaos. The Act will start unraveling the fabric of Indian family life," said Maa Ghara Foundation trustee.

She also stated that it would give rise to child pregnancy and has far reaching ramifications, adding despite its aim to restrict multiple partners; it would have an adverse impact on the youths and result in the spread of HIV / AIDS.

"Children, born out of living together relationships, would not be properly brought up," the trustee added.

She further said that the transition of the Indian families, from the clan to joint family and then nuclear family and now 'living together' looks to be a gradual minimisation of the family structure and time spent.

Social scientists have already identified grave social problems like young age pregnancy of adolescent girls, drug abuse, violence and juvenile delinquencies and in the wake of the controversial ruling, the erstwhile objectionable social behaviour gets legalised, many felt.

The NGO reiterated that prior to the introduction of the controversial Live-in Relationship, the Government should amend the Hindu Marriage Act, Hindu Succession Act, Hindu Joint Family Property Act et al, modify existing Pension Schemes, Rehabilitation Schemes, Reservation Rights, Medical Benefits, modify and amend the Indian Penal Code and other Acts relating to women, set up a Registration Authority to check fraudulent relationships and also set up a competent authority for rehabilitation in case of divorce or desertion by a partner.

In case of a divorce or death of husband, the wife is the legal heir to the parental property for maintaining her as well as her children's livelihood. In case of live-in relationship, the family may not accept the bond and debar from the very right of succession. Deprived of the rights, one cannot take recourse to the legal shelter to prove the rights in the ambits of the prevalent Hindu Succession Act. Moreover, the Government also may not allow the other benefits admissible to the Government employees.

Samantha Wetherbee, Ohio, United States - I live in Ohio, U S. and our culture is very bizarre about these issues. Sex is promoted everywhere, and then culture gets unexpectedly Puritanical from time to time.

What I've seen is that as women become more "free" about their sexuality, men do not become better people all of a sudden. Instead of being respected as a free individual, women are expected to perform all sorts of sex acts with men without expecting anything from the men. So the "sexual revolution" means that men get all sorts of benefits and nothing expected of them, while women get taken advantage of.

In our schools, teenage boys expect girls to send them nude pictures on their cell phones so they can see if the girl is worth dating (it's illegal to send nude pictures of someone under 18 years of age, and some girls have been charged with crimes and are now registered "sex offenders" for these pictures of themselves - this means that for the rest of their lives, their neighbors will be alerted when they move in that a sex offender lives in the neighborhood).

Men think nothing of asking women for certain sexual favours when they aren't even in a relationship...favours the woman really gets nothing out of (I mean, heck, Bill Clinton said it's not really "sexual relations" so it's no big deal).

Has crime against women and girls diminished? Not at all! Every single week I see another little girl in the news, kidnapped, raped and thrown away in the woods, a dumpster, a lake. If you talk to adult women, in a group of 20 or 30 you might find 1 or 2 who have never been raped or molested. If you're lucky!

So in our culture it's not illegal to have pre-marital sex or a live-in relationship. In fact, it's encouraged. But it hasn't made the deeper problems go away. Feminism is a long, hard road and I honestly don't know when we'll get the freedoms and respect that men have.

I have heard this in a few developing religious cultures; the view that women somehow hold the cashier register to the "sexual gratification" shop. Meaning sex is to be given away to get something in return (anything ranging from relationship to financial security.) Now this bothers me as any well-adjusted individual should be able to recognise and satiate their physiological needs without causing harm to another. How about understanding that sometimes women want just that... no more no less? I also whole heartedly agree on respecting one's body and spirit for all its worth and that applies to men and women. This whole mind game played on both sides (presumably men for sex and women for financial or moral security) bothers me.

Women everywhere should be financially and even more, emotionally strong and they should love themselves and respect themselves enough to reject any relationships that don't value them.

Materialistic societies are based on men wanting objects and women wanting to become objects. "Instead of being respected as a free individual, women are expected to perform all sorts of sex acts with men without expecting anything from the men." - This is exactly what is promoted on cable networks in the West.

A woman should know she is important - as important as the next person. Every girl needs to understand that. Indian girls need to know this even more... because nobody else believes her - after all she should be counting her blessings that she is even born.

Hemali Shah, Surat, Gujarat - That the esteemed judges of the Supreme Court (SC) impulsively brought in the example of Radha and Krishna is totally uncalled for. People at such high positions are not expected to make statements on a subject on which they themselves are not clear. Goddess Radha had a single pointed devotion towards Lord Krishna, an example of unconditional love in its purest form.

This is how you revere your Goddess, by dragging her to court, and to just justify an act which we all know (agree or disagree) is cent percent unethical and immoral? It is totally unacceptable and inappropriate. The court could have simply said that as per existing laws, living-in does not constitute an offense. It is for the legislature to bring in appropriate legislation. And such laws are always rooted in the cultural and moral values practiced in society at that point of time. I cannot quote my ancestors in caves to justify using a club (wooden or stone) on a woman.

To bring in such pure relationships to justify the modern generation's uncontrolled infatuation and their total unconcern to moral principles shows their ignorance about their own scriptures and even lack of common sense. The judges are requested not to make such irresponsible comments and certainly not relating to any religion, while dealing the cases in future. Please maintain the high values and the standards of the Supreme Court.

First it was the gays and homos OK decision...now it's the pre-marital sex OK ...What's it gonna be next?

Santosh Ganjoo, Udhampur, J&K, India - Live-in relationships is absolutely a wrong move. It is a decision taken by immature, insecure and irresponsible people, who have no respect for our great culture and heritage. They are people who shy away from their responsibilities and who are incapable of taking a firm stand in life.

It is ridiculous to refer to Radha and Lord Krishna in the judgement relating to live-in relationships. The statement as reported in the media: "Drawing an analogy from the Hindu mythology, even Lord Krishna and Radha lived together" cannot be and should not be accepted by any Hindu.

We are utterly flabbergasted at the misuse of Radha-Krishna relationship in support of this techno-legal judgement. What was the need for such a reference? The case would have stood by itself on merit based on liberal democratic values within the framework of the Indian constitution.

It is the Jury's mischaracterisation of the Radha-Krishna relationship that amounts to a brutal assault on the Hindu traditions and culture, exacerbated by the fact that they are the highest judicial authority in the country. It would be absurd to take Radha-Krishna relationship this as a live-in relationship as the term is understood in modern parlance.

Humans invented the institution of marriage to fulfill the basic purpose of human existence. This institution has survived tribulations of time and across all cultures of the world. The excessive materialistic culture of West with its non-responsible unfettered individualism as the social driver, led to the break-down of the family structure, resulting in high divorce rates, teen-pregnancies, child abandonment, along with the so called live-in relationships. As an inarticulate backlash against such unconventional social arrangements, the conservatives all over the world have vilified the practitioners of alternate lifestyles. The conservative backlash and vilification is to be unambiguously condemned. Where does Radha-Krishna relationship fit into this equation?

As per the Hindu beliefs, the relationship between Radha and Krishna symbolises cosmic love. The same cosmic love was experienced by Meera (an unparalleled devotee of Lord Krishna) by her unequivocal devotion to Lord Krishna. Would you characterise Meera and Krishna relationship as also sexual?

The problem with "modern" types is that they evaluate cultural history and traditions by their faulty Western-inspired materialistic lenses, where everything is about bodily fulfillment. Where the parameters of human existence is limited to filling the stomach with food, numbing the senses with alcohol, the physical act of obtaining an orgasm, and then turning over and trying to get some sleep. Basically just live the life of an animal. With such parameters it is difficult to understand Radha-Krishna relationship. This is the precise reason you should have left Radha and Krishna alone in your adjudication process.

Muhammed Aftab, Lalganj, Bihar - It is quite true that live-in relationships have found a place in Indian society. I personally may not like the system but one has to accept the fact that soon they are to become integral part of our society. However, I still believe marriage is far better and intelligent option to adopt! You can't fully rely on your cohabiting partner. Moral values make each person different.

Living together without being married cannot be detached from morals. This is not at all a good concept for a human being, we people are not here only for food, sex and money... apart from that a lot of things we have to do. We should not indulge in this type of relationship such a concept is unethical, immoral and bad. Allah permits a boy and a girl (if they like each other) only to marry first and then stay together, not vice-versa.

Vineet Mashroo, Shimla - This is what I feel - I don't approve of live-ins. I have seen my friends do it - some successfully and some not.

I think that the convenience of a live-in relationship doesn't make the couple responsible towards themselves and their relationship. It's open ended and a walk-out is generally easy, which is a good thing considering violence, rape etc. etc. But, it's also a way of escaping commitment on a permanent basis.

Once committed, I don't find why a live-in is needed, marriage works just as fine (call me old-fashioned, but this is me). And one needs to work towards a marriage, but in a live-in, maybe, not so much. A small fight or ego hassle could be the reason for a breakup, whereas marriage allows one to introspect and change (one self or spouse).

Now, pre-marital sex is no one's business. Whether it is the man or woman - it's nobody's business, and asking whether the partner is a virgin or not is stupid. As long as one isn't cheating on the partner, the past shouldn't matter. Comparing partners is also foolish, because the sex is always the best with the person you are in love with. So, if you have fallen in love more than once, then you are lucky enough to have amazing sex with more than one person.

Unfortunately, in our country especially, one doesn't view it like this. While men are put on a pedestal for having "scored", women are generally crucified for "doing it" outside "marriage".

My question is why are our Indian men so insecure? It is insecurity and the false ego which makes them behave like Neanderthals (primitive, uncivilised) when it comes to sex and women. Also, we are the biggest bunch of hypocrites to have ever walked on Mother Earth! We condemn and call dirty something which gives life, which keeps your heart rate up and also makes sure you are happy.

How many times have we heard - "He / She needs a good lay, and then he / she will be alright"? How many colleagues or friends have we seen frustrated (especially men) because they aren't getting any action?

I think we need to raise our children better. It always starts at home. Education starts at home. If the children see their parents holding hands, or hugging or even sharing a kiss, they know it's a beautiful way to express love and they will with time and maturity understand that sex is a good thing and not bad or dirty!

Whether live-ins or the pre-marital sex - one should know what it involves, the responsibilities and the consequences. And as long as the partners are in sync, it shouldn't matter to the outside world!

Preetinder Singh, Delhi - I believe in social security, family bonding and after all marriage followed by living together. An adult definitely should choose his or her partner.

But pre-marital sex and living together without recognition from the family members will disrupt the relationship and ethics of our Indian culture.

Before opting for such a relationship one should think about its social acceptance. As the rapes are not socially accepted and hence are considered offensive and punishable then why not cohabiting. If you can create the acceptance for these things, you win.

Xavier Abraham, Kodala, Orissa - Khushboo expressed her personal opinion. I expected the court would just uphold her right to endorse anything, for we can't police a man's thought process! Instead, the court went one step ahead to share her opinion. Is it that our judiciary wants to express its opinion on everything under the sun?

Why call it live-in relationship, call it free sex society, its strange, we people adore these people from the film industry, elect them to parliament, give them hoards of money to spend lavishly, just because we can't resist their charm and run after them like mad dogs. This is the value-less relationship, which has no future.

Dominick Donaghy, Walhalla, Victoria - I detest live-in relationships. It is a disease. Living with someone before marriage is not a true "marriage before marriage" experience. That is a myth. As long as there is not true commitment involved, a relationship cannot be like a marriage. A true commitment involves not being afraid to sign a paper stating that you wili stay with that person, regardless, for the rest of your life. People think that if you have lived together for a long time, you can turn it into marriage. That is not true, unless you have been able to work out compromises and solutions to your problems, and have incorporated all chores, responsibilities, finances, etc. into one total. Becoming one the big issue. After marriage, your lives, although somewhat separate for various activities, becomes one over all. None of that happens when you live together. There is always an open door to leave, if you are unhappy. That door closes when you get married, and 'THAT' scares some people so badly that they end up ruining what was previously a comfortable relationship. I see it happen all of the time.

The only time that just living together as a couple should happen is after a person has grown older and is not going to be having any more children. The children born out of wedlock are the ones that always suffer. Who are we to make a child's life miserable? If we cannot even try or dare to commit in marriage, we should not be having a child? It is premeditated abuse of a child.

By the way, having sex does not necessarily have anything to do with love. It is just more intense and emotionally enjoyable when a couple is in love. As long as they are protecting from disease and pregnancy, then how they live their lives is up to them, because it only affects them.

Nehal Hinduja, Raipur, India - Is pre-marital sex even an issue for the highest court to debate? Indians are crying for resolution of key constitutional questions over reservation, freedom of expression, taxation, property ownership, equal treatment under law, and religion.

Indians are crying for relief from corrupt government, exploitative corporations (including media corporations), crooked middlemen.

Uchchpal Singh Riar, Jammu - Those who are actually appreciating and welcoming this decision have no long term view, they are only seeing it from the lens of personal and individualistic experience, not from the view of what is actually beneficial for the society. They are unaware of the social disaster and degradation such alien concepts have introduced in the West - indeed West is on a moral decline in spite of having progressed so much materially. When certain bunch of people are welcoming it, it's only because of the fact that they feel that emulating the West in this and other matters is the only way India can be "prosperous" (in Western sense).

They are more interested in enjoying their rights rather than be responsible towards their society and values. In the days of freedom struggle, we had individuals who even did not hesitate to sacrifice their lives for the sake of freedom - now we have people who are not even able to responsibly contribute - so much for sacrificing! Instead of blindly aping the West in these matters individuals should see the observation in its depth, its impact in West and evaluate it critically before even commenting on it. It's unfortunate that even the courts did not take such a view.

Court can change its decision and give a credit to live-in relationship but it won't be able to change people's perspective about such relationship. This decision takes our society and culture one step closer to destruction.

Rameshraju, India - Sex before marriage surely ruins the Indian Family system. The Supreme Court's judgement destroys the Indian culture. It causes the institution of marriage to vanish gradually. Women are the ultimate victims of this judgement. This judgement also results in praise of Prostitution and teen pregnancy. I think the Supreme Court judges should be stoned to death for giving this insane judgement. It is time for us to save our culture from damnation.

Supreme Court's judgement is absurd and insane. Sex before marriage surely harms Indian culture. It mainly destroys the institution of marriage gradually. Most men of today prefer marriage to have sex life. If a man tastes a woman, and if he is not satisfied, he may leave her in the lurch. Sex before marriage may result in teen pregnancy. It is not wise to take example from Indian mythology. At the time of Vedas, Incest was practiced. In future Supreme Court may say that Incest is no crime. I think Supreme Court judges are true traitors - because they are trying to harm Indian culture. It is time to save our culture. It is better to protest against Supreme Court to ban sex before marriage, same sex marriage etc.

Sex before marriage is termed as Fornication. It destroys Indian culture. Fornication and Incest were existed prior to Vedic period. But they were banned to prevent unwanted pregnancy, to prevent women from being cheated by men, to strengthen marriage institution and family system. Taking examples from Puranas (Indian sacred books in Sanskrit literature) is insane. In Matsya Purana, Brahma married his own daughter Saraswathi. What if Supreme Court says Incest too is no wrong? Women are the ultimate victims of fornication. Legalisation of fornication rapidly increases prostitution. It helps men and women to escape easily from police rides. Fornication is a form of prostitution. It ruins family system and marriage institution and ultimately Indian society.

Jagraj Singh Malhi, Essex, U.K. - The tragedy in our country is the law which can allow 22 criminal cases to be filed against a lady for some trivial statement and it can come up in the highest court in the land so that some judge can enjoy his 15 minutes (and extend that to 15 years). Hope you are happy Mr. Ambedkar. The retards, led by this dude, added considerable amount of ambiguity in almost every law and the result is that the lawyers and judges are enjoying themselves.

We definitely need to relook compensation for judges ... pay them by how many cases they clear or the better criteria can be the social importance of the cases and also the time spent (rather wasted) on the cases taken up for hearing.

Pankaj Advani, Bhilai, Chhattisgarh - The concept is very unethical and definitely going to harm the women in the long run. God knows who revealed to the Honourable Jury all these very personal and private secrets of these revered and iconic figures. But the statement had all the power to really tarnish their image and making mockery of Hindu Gods all around the world. It was not at all necessary for the Honourable Supreme Court of India to give any example as in the cases of molestations and rapes no Court quotes the Kings of the past (even after understanding the meanings given in our Mythological Books which have hinted in this direction in very humble languages). Even if it was found by the jury necessary to put forward some example to clarify its point then instead of Radha-Krishna relationship, they could have better quoted some proved cases which are already known to the modern world (for example as that of Shakuntla and King Dushyanta).

Taufiqne A. Al-Abbasi, Buraydah, Saudi Arabia – Recently the Supreme Court of India has legalised the live-in relationship. It is not a crime but the age factor should be added to it rather than giving its approval blindly to all the citizens.

I know sex is natural desire which grows in teenage years till death and should be fulfilled. I find today people going for live-in relationship with a person for a period and after that they marry some other person. An experience of marriage before marriage I think for above 25 years of age is fine but for less than 25 it is too lusty. I think where there is true love there is no known sexual desire.

Parimal Dash, Bhubhaneswar, India - The relationship between Radha and Krishna was not live together. It shows very poorly that Chief Justice Of India is completely unaware of mythical, philosophical currents of the country but make comments that are not only false, but can outrage people as well. Why always selectively distort Hindu traditions? Some people are approaching court on reference made to Radha-Krishna by CJI. So, he should apologise for his comments on the two highly worshipped figures. It's a serious matter to most Indians.

I don't support Rama Sena type violence (latest update on that states it was sponsored by underworld). But in the name of freedom, total anarchy can't be allowed either. The only fear of any right or Law per say in the Indian Scenario is the exploitation and abuse of the same. It's a good thing that one could lawfully do it now, but with that comes a greater responsibility, and I really am apprehensive, if that would be understood the way it is meant to be with our kind of political and social background. The idea is full of risks particularly for the fairer sex.

Much of West's problems come from so called total freedom of sex. People are not marrying, birth rate have fallen drastically in many countries, or massive changes taking place in demography that will change the underlying religio-cultural values of the Europe. When basic building blocks of society (marriage, family) are corrupted then, no house built on that can sustain.

Teenaged sex / pre-marital sex have caused massive social problems in the West. It was not so even few decades back. Now, more children are born outside wedlock in the US. There is huge problem in bringing them up as good, normal citizens. If a child is not brought up properly, it affects their future mental buildup, education etc. as well as their role as parents. It's a cycle that is impossible to break.

Zia Ul Naqvi, Pakistan - Live-in relationship is neither legal nor ethical but recent opinions and judgements from Indian judiciary show that there cannot be any objection from their side if two adults of opposite sex start living together without marrying each other. But, one point everyone should consider is that it is women who would be in loss in live-in relationship and not men. Also, the breaking down of family system would have damaging effect on the society. Law cannot do much in this and similar other trends which occur according to the developments in the particular society. When two likeminded people of opposite sex are living together no government or judiciary can ask them to live separate for they are not married to each other.

To my understanding, live-in relationship would catch the mainstream in coming days. More the women start earning, more will they be independent and free thinkers. On the other hand, men with average earning would not be able to manage full-fledged marriage and would resort to ad-hoc arrangements, i.e. live-in relationships. As long as the trend would not disturb the system of the society, there would not be any landmark uproar against it. So, live-in relationship is to stay here for some time but cannot be substituted for marriage.

Enlai Zhang, Shanghai - How can such relationship be morally acceptable? Although this is individual choice to lead the life the way one wishes, yet, our society (particularly Asian) does not approve this relationship. Something weird about live-in relationship is that when two like-minded mature adults can stay together then what is the obstacle in adhering to the social norms?

Ultimately in an arranged or love marriage also, two individuals get engaged after properly evaluating each other in view of understanding family backgrounds or having accommodated with each other's family because of their liking to each other.

The compatibility, feeling something special about somebody only is the root cause of all the marriage proposals, therefore those who appreciate each other and wish to spend their lives under one roof need to deliberate that no relationship has a long life unless intense feeling, love, sacrifice, responsibility, attachment, or interest in each other exists. Relationship, be it friendship even cannot change instantly with whims and fancies. Moreover such trend, the one like live-in relationship influence others to imitate without proper pondering over the repercussions. Live-in relationship may prove to be a bad precedent.

11
Do Live-In Relationships Work?

Many say 'YES'

Kriszia Vengua, Nauwle, South Africa - Think about it: you can test drive a car, so why not test drive a relationship?

Magazines come with 30 day trials; we have return policies for electronics, and free samples for ice cream. So why can't we get the same money back guarantee with our relationships?

The answer is that we do. They're called live-in relationships. It's a brilliant idea that makes perfect sense but unfortunately, doesn't work.

That's because by the large number of married couples and those who live together both want the same things: commitment. The idea of sharing the rest of your life with someone, with all its ups and downs, is what makes being in a relationship so rewarding, something, which living together doesn't quite lend itself to.

Successful partnerships are built on a series of compromises; something that is severely undermined when your only intention is to stay with that person so long as they keep you happy. It's not that marriages are meant to be unhappy, but that it realises that happiness is fleeting. It comes and it goes.

Beyond the signed documents, marriage forces you to look at the long term. When you think about the rest of your life, you're more than willing to make sacrifices in order to stay together. If putting the toilet seat up is an argument that's likely to occur for the rest of your married life, then you might learn to just put it down yourself...then back up after you've used it. Likewise, if doing a bit more of the chores are going to keep her from whining for the next fifty years, then you'd be more inclined to do the dishes.

This doesn't happen as much with live-in couples. When you're living together, your concern isn't with what's good for your marriage; it's rather what's good for yourself. You're searching for something that's going to suit you, which is pretty much the case what you're doing when you test drive a car.

People aren't cars, in the same way that they aren't magazines or free samples. That car will still behave like a car from the moment you take it for a test spin to the time it hits the junk yard. A magazine will still have the same content even after your 30 day trial. In the same way that an ice cream will never change whether or not you tried the sampler.

People aren't as predictable. How they are in the first three years won't be the same as the next ten or twenty. So when your idea of "for better or worse" changes into "only for the better", then you won't likely stay around for when things come from worse back to better.

The idea of being with a person day in and day out is that you'll know what they're like. You can only know what's like to be married to someone when you actually are married to them, that's why less than 50 percent of live-in couples make it to the altar. And those who are more than likely to divorce. They notice that marriage is extremely different from living together, after knowing what it really is like to face a lifelong commitment. That's why most struggle to even make it past the seven year itch.

The average live-in rate is two years. If you're willing to go through life testing one live-in relationship after another, then you might one day discover that it's too late. So instead of settling for a string of fake commitments, why not bite the bullet and try the real thing once?

Sangeetha J., Trichi, India - Live-in relationships are a growing trend in youngsters of India, especially in the metros cities. Like wedding portals, nowadays we have a tendency to also have live-in relationship portals. I'm sure this trend existed even decades back but then at that time it should have been a hushed-hushed affair. Even these days, going by the social trends in India not several people are ready to accept these kinds of relationships open heartedly. In metros live-in relationships these days are simply as common as having a spouse or a fiancee. Still, such couples would rather not accept it in public in India, barring simply a few.

One issue that everybody wonders though is why do couples like such relationships to marriage? Is it being practical or simply convenience? Does it depict individuality or in a very larger perspective, is it one amongst the numerous trends that have caught on to us from the West?

Marriage demands a lot of affection, dedication, responsibility and commitment. Both the couples coming from completely different backgrounds have to really strive arduous and modify to each different to make it work. It's a widely known truth that youngsters, especially guys, do get cold feet by just the mere thought of marriage. It's not just regarding living along and sharing an apartment however sharing each others' life, joys and sorrows. But still there can be instances when even once attempting their best things would possibly simply not work.

Boys and girls nowadays go in for live-in relationships, as they wish to make certain that they are compatible with each other and would be ready to stay the remainder of their lives together. Some simply need to check the waters before taking the plunge. For some "Live-in relationship is sort of a check drive". Whereas others actually don't need the commitment and responsibility as a wedding demands between them. Live-in relationship for them is a straightforward approach out. Living in for some means enjoying all the togetherness a marriage provides however with no strings attached. Moreover there are no legal hassles for separation if the couples attempt to half ways, not like marriage. This may ultimately have both its benefits and drawbacks, as there is no legal method out if one amongst the partners cheats the other as such relationships in India are still not legally accepted. Though additional than half-of the couples do finish up getting married, it might be as emotionally devastating to the remainder of the couples as it is for couples with failed marriages. After all, nobody will be that sensible when it involves emotions. But time proves to be the final healer in such cases as well.

So what's higher, wedding or a live-in relationship? Really this discussion can last for long with no definite conclusions. For my part, couples getting in for live-in relationships should be certain of what they want out of this arrangement. Is it a short lived factor or if they would ultimately want to take the link forward. In the former case, it's a lot of like space mates and they have to have clear ground rules, on who will what. In the later case however, it's as smart as living as a married couple and so it ought to also be given the same kind of dedication, love and commitment which a wedding demands. What very matters at the end of the day is not what name is given to a relationship, however how robust the bond between them is, emotionally and if they can extremely face the ups and downs of life - together.

We can quote the number of Ayes and Nays as there are people who don't take live-in relationship seriously and believe that it does not work in the long run, but there are many who take only this relationship seriously and have full faith in the "Institution of Cohabitation".

Christina A. Armani, Florence, Italy – Live-in relationships do work but it really does depend on the couple. We live in a modern society, so there is nothing wrong with a couple living together. I have lived with my fiancee since the summer of 2005 and we're doing fine as a couple. It may not be a picnic all the time, but we love seeing each other all the time and not having to pay for two separate places. Most relationships end up not work out regardless of the living arrangements.

Life is short so why not enjoy living with your boyfriend or girlfriend? The truth is that most marriages don't work out now a day. With the divorce rates being so high in many places all over the world, living together is a lot less risky. Live-in relationships bring couples closer together, or they help them realise that the relationship is a mistake before it goes too far.

Living together isn't right for every couple, but you get to know the person really well. You even get to know what they would be like if you were married to them. Many divorces could be spared if the couple lived together first, even if it was just for a month or two. When you live with the person you love, you learn everything you would ever want to know about them.

Live-in relationships are hard work but so is marriage. Live-in relationships are a good way to prepare for marriage and know what to expect from marriage. If you're not ready to have a live-in relationship yet, then it's definitely too soon for you to be thinking about getting married. If you do decide to have a live-in relationship, it won't work if you do it for the wrong reasons. You should do it because you want to, not because you want to move away from your parents or change up a mundane life or because you feel pressured to.

Living together is not a decision to rush into or take lightly. It's not something to be impulsive about, but if you have really thought about it and think it is a good idea, then move in already! Live-in relationships only work if you take the time and effort to make them work. Living together requires hard work and commitment; it is not all fun and games. It takes a lot of determination and dedication to make a relationship work, and if living together feels right for you then go for it.

Mel Bergen, Sydney, Australia - Live-in relationships can work, yes, but they often do not. It's a question of the stability of the relationship and the commitment of the partners.

Leaping into a live-in situation is never a good idea. You should be close to your significant other and should know each other well. Take a look at where they live now - do they have habits that will drive you nuts? Are you constantly picking up things for them (or they for you)? How do they squeeze that toothpaste tube? Do they forget to call when they're going to be late or do they have a heart attack when you get home from work 10 minutes later than usual? Can you live with these things?

Then consider your own lifestyle. Think about having someone there to know and care when you come and go. Don't forget to take into account whether you get along with each other's friends, as well. Having your best friend over twice a week when your partner can't stand to see him or her will strain relations indeed, on both sides.

Then there are the living arrangements. If you have roommates now, will your partner move in with you or the other way around, or will you find a new place? Unless you own your home, you'll have to sign a new lease. Moving someone into your flat without one could get you evicted. Think about how well you've gotten along with your roommates, now or in the past. Are you ready to share your space (not just the bathroom but your bedroom as well) with someone full-time? Can you give up your privacy and having a retreat during difficult times?

These are all questions you should ask yourself whether you are contemplating only moving in together or getting married as well. There isn't much difference in your day-to-day life between the two - a live-in romantic relationship ought to be a step on the road to a lifetime commitment. But I'm living a proof that live-in relationships work. My husband and I have been partners for 10 years, have lived together for 8, and have been married for 7 months. We may be a little slow, but we're surer than most couples who get married without ever sharing living space.

Valerie Langton, Marseille, France - The issue of live-in relationships depends on the personalities and beliefs of the people involved in the relationship itself. In my experience, live-in relationships are good for several reasons:

1. You can only know what a person is truly like when you live with them day-in and day-out. For example, before my boyfriend and I lived together, I had no clue that he could get toothpaste literally 'EVERYWHERE' (I'm not kidding – I've found toothpaste on the STOVE!) Fortunately, that is a quirk that I can live with, but what if it had been something worse, something that I could not live with, and I hadn't been able to find out until marriage? Would I have to spend the rest of my life dealing with something that I couldn't tolerate? This leads me to number 2:

2. Its much more expensive and painful to get a divorce than it is to end a dating relationship (even a serious one). Divorces hurt people's credit ratings, their financial situation, and their emotional states, among other things. If there are children involved, it can be even worse.

3. If he "buys the cow" after "getting the milk for free", that must mean that there's more to your relationship than the wanting of intercourse. Maybe even something like love and devotion. NOTE: I am, in no way knocking people who wait until marriage to have sex. Many of my very best friends chose this course and are now happily married. It is not the course of life for everyone, however, and they also acknowledge this and accept the choices of others.

4. This goes back to number 1, but you can find out if you are able to live together, and then you don't have to ruin your honey moon deciding where his/her clothes should go and where to hang that awful picture of Mr. ABC they've brought with them.

5. Marriage will still change things for you, but by that time you'll have already gone through so much together that it won't bother you as much. Sure, there will still be fights,

but if you can make it through them unscathed, your relationship will be much stronger.

It is not that all live-in-relationships will lead to marriage, but that's sort of the point, isn't it? Much of the reason, I invited my boyfriend to live with me is, so that we could find out if we were compatible enough to make the next step. I believe, we are.

Jeanne Roux, Le Mans, France - As my mother and grandmother used to say, "Why buy the cow, when you can get the milk for free?" This was a not-so-flattering analogy to a "living together" arrangement, instead of marriage.

When I was a kid, it was interesting to see the different terms people came up with to describe their live-in lover: Cohabitant, POSSLQ (Person of Opposite Sex Sharing Living Quarters), Significant Other (SO), Lover, Friend, Boyfriend / Girlfriend (though they are more than that), Fiancee.

I lived with someone for 6 years, despite of my faith's approval. He fluctuated between boyfriend and fiancee, depending on the status of the mercurial relationship. Of course it could be argued that if it was mercurial, why stay in the relationship? I argued that since it was mercurial, it was wise to go no further.

Studies seem to indicate that living together is not as healthy as marriage. But what they fail to examine is 'WHY'. It is often said (or implied) that problems come from living together. Yet, in my opinion (based on self experience and the experience of others) living together comes from problems. If the problems didn't exist, marriage would occur. Instead, the partners exist in relationship purgatory.

One obvious solution is to avoid being involved with someone if there are problems which would impede marriage. But it starts with "We'll be OK once we get this one little thing ironed out," and it escalates when the "one little thing" multiplies like nymphomaniac rabbits.

Of course keeping sex out of the relationship before marriage, discourages living together, which helps you evaluate the situation from a distance for a while. But the problem with evaluating something from a distance is that you may never discover the problem until you are married.

In a recent study to probe the minds of America's young men, aged 25 to 33, the study found 10 reasons men won't commit - from the ease of finding sex partners to the desire to avoid financial risks of divorce.

Why buy the cow, when you can get the milk for free?

But we also need to realise that women are equally to blame in this. Despite the fact that young men are reluctant to commit, it's the young women who are offering up the milk (so to speak). And, as the study points out, "[The men] love their single life and experience few of the traditional pressures from church, employers or society that once encouraged them to marry."

It also should be pointed out that the study took place in major metropolitan areas; Chicago, New Jersey, Washington, D.C. and Houston. It is undoubtedly true that cohabitation is seen distasteful in rural areas.

However, the study makes an assertion that I would like to see backed up with facts: "Marriage is a fundamental social institution. It is central to the nurture and rearing of children... and the 'social glue' that reliably attaches fathers to children," noted in the report. "[Marriage] contributes to the physical, emotional and economic health of men, women and children, and thus to the nation as a whole."

In a relationship where the partners are equally committed, what is the difference between marriage and cohabitation? Of course, I come from the perspective of living in a No Fault Divorce state. If your partner wants out, he's out, whether you like it or not. And if the reason for divorce is that he has sex with multiple partners or a circus goat named Billy, it doesn't matter in the least. In states where Fault Divorce is allowed, perhaps marriage holds more value.

If you have valuable assets and you wish to protect them, you have the uncomfortable agony of asking (or forcing) your fiancee to sign a prenupital agreement to protect those assets. Oh sure, "the glory of love" is a beautiful thing and it's easy to neglect the warning signs until he walks off with half of your hard-earned estate when things doesn't work out. Isn't it easier to spare yourself the court battles and the troubles?

So, (at least in Florida where No Fault Divorce reigns, and there's no such thing as Common Law Marriage) why should they buy the cow when they can get the milk for free?

Is this the de-evolving or evolving of a society? Will this push us toward strict divorce laws to show that we take marriage seriously? And will that be better or worse for us as a society? It is unlikely that we can change hearts and minds in order to create a society where marriage is valued once again. To use another of my mom's phrases, "we're shutting the barn door after the horse got out."

Rehana Majeed, Hong Kong – Live-in relationships are what you make out of them. The choice to move in with someone is not always an easy one. To make things work it is a good idea to talk about some guidelines. For example-how do you feel about other friends spending the night, when is it too late to have someone over or call, are there any things you just can't stand such as laundry on the floor. These things may not seem like a big deal but when dealing with them everyday, small things add up!

I also suggest that before marrying one should someone live with the person for one year. This may sound silly but I promise you, it is good advice! People change their behavior and mannerisms when they are truly comfortable with living with someone. Often you will see things that you didn't see when you were dating; this could include behaviors, habits, or mannerisms. How people react and act during the holidays is important to know as well. For example your partner may seem really helpful now but when festivals and other occasions come around are they going to do their share? Will you do all the shopping yourself? Cooking? Your traditions for each holiday could be totally different and neither of you may want to compromise. Wouldn't you want to know before you walked down the aisle?

I had a wonderful partner whom I dated for almost 5 years and we truly loved each other. We decided to move in together and it was a nightmare! I couldn't stand his messiness and lack of organisation! He thought since we were living together that I would cook and clean for him. It just didn't work out so we had to break up. I thank God that I didn't get married and then move in together. I know this doesn't happen to everyone but wouldn't you want to be sure before you are committed yourselves till 'death'?

Gayatri Tambe, Thane, Maharashtra, India Relationships only work if the people are meant to be together and are ready and willing to put some work into the relationship. Nothing thrives without love.

While living-in may be liberating for some women, social research proves otherwise. Women have to be extra careful and need to be very clear about why they choose to cohabitate with a partner. A woman must ask herself whether cohabitation a way of minimising the risk of divorce, or is it seen as a cheap and easy alternative to marriage?

In cohabitation, you need to start with your eyes wide open. Before shifting in with a man, consider, why you are doing it. Is it because you want it, or is it because it will make it more convenient, or is it the all-crucial "moving it to the next level"?

Women must analyse a situation and examine possible interpretations of what this move may mean and what implications this is going to have on the state of the relationship, both now and in the times to come. Most men simply see it as somewhere pretty to stick your stuff and to be nurtured and don't think too much into the future.

Live-in relationships can become a healthy marriage. As with any relationship it must be nurtured. I grew up believing that living in with someone is a sin. I won't dispute this but I did let my boyfriend move in with me. We got married less than a year later. We were engaged for over six months and went through the course that the law and religion requires if you are going to get married. We practiced abstinence before our marriage. We are now happily married with two beautiful babies.

Marriages without living together can fall apart. I have a sister that didn't live with her fiancee before they were married. They also were engaged for more than six months and were divorced within six months after their marriage.

Marriages without living together can thrive. My parents, who knew each other for years and didn't move in together, they were happily married with three kids, until my dad passed away. They were married for thirty five years.

When live-in relationships first came out in open in India, it created a storm and was accused of being against Indian morality and culture. As the decades have gone by, the number of couples opting for cohabitation, without the strings of marriage, has increased significantly.

It became a trend that is more evident in the last decade. That the Indian government who have recently recognised live-in relationships on par with marriage, in a new law on Domestic Violence, proves that this is a growing social reality. Live-in relationships may have attained legal recognition, despite the controversies surrounding it but whether it has social acceptance, is another issue altogether. No doubt, we are global in our outlook in many ways; our society does frown upon live-in relationships.

Although Most Indians believe that a man and woman can only live under the same roof and share a bed if they are married to each other, but for the younger generation, who are more influenced by the Western Culture and those who have lived abroad, it is more acceptable.

It is believed that married couples make an attempt to compromise and accommodate to each other's life because the marriage is supposed to last for life. Cohabiting couples don't do this because they don't have a life-long commitment. Different people, different results.

Kerry Hosking, Longwood, Florida - Does one need follow the others these days? You meet someone special, start dating, become engaged, get married and go off to work or finish college, and then you start a family. Are all the steps necessary or can we skip the engagement and vows, and slot the baby somewhere in the middle?

People get married most of the time, not only because they are in love, but because that is what their parents and grandparents did. We all want to follow tradition if it is symbolised by long lasting, happy relationships that our families have enjoyed. Many of us have been raised in this type of situation; however, it's not reason enough to call the wedding planner or spend thousands on a wedding gown. There are unhealthy reasons for getting married, too.

Getting married because of an unexpected pregnancy is an unhealthy reason to get wed, as can be marrying purely for financial reasons.

It would seem that there are more healthy reasons for cohabitation, and none unhealthy - at least that's what my observations indicated until I chose to live in another country. In Australia, de-facto relationships are the norm, and lots of people never get married. The reason most don't bother can vary; de-facto relationships are recognised by the law in Australia, and the spouse is entitled to health benefits, social security, retirement benefits from their spouse, and proceeds of a will assigned to a legal partner, whether married or not.

Here in the U.S., there are numerous problems for people who live together without being married. Most of the benefits mentioned are not automatically granted to a de-facto spouse in the event of death or separation, and overall, people seem to be more religious and cohabitation is frowned upon by some religions. Children can also be disadvantaged due to the lack of legal commitment by their parents.

Some people can live together for a very long time without being engaged or married, and as soon as they make that commitment, disaster can follow shortly afterward. One would be inclined to think that this is more of a psychological problem. Perhaps we think we are somehow more tied to one place or person if we get married, than if we live with that person as a de-facto. If an unmarried union is working well, it is unhealthy to get married 'just because of what other people may think'. These days, people get married; both go to college, and raise kids. It can be done, but keep in mind that it can be unhealthy to wait too long to have children; more babies are born with birth defects to older parents.

Chenault De Salis, Toulon, France - As with all other relationships, you get what you give. In a situation of living together while dating you will find out if you are really compatible. Living together in my opinion, is a great idea before marriage. You will know what you are getting into, you will find out how strong your relationship really is. If you can't get along in a live-in relationship, you should definitely not consider marriage!

When I rented my first house, my boyfriend was as happy as I was about my new living situation. He was at my house each day after work, he frequently slept over, and in general he got comfortable at my house. I suggested him to move in with me. He declined and said he didn't want to take over my home. Within three weeks, he started bringing clothes, videos and furniture over. He was moving in.

It was perfect at first. It seemed like a honeymoon. We ate dinner together, we woke up together, we had lots of time to cuddle and make love. We were very happy. After two months, the honeymoon was over. We had to learn to accommodate one another, and make our situation work. We had our differences, such as household chores. I didn't feel that I should be responsible for his laundry; I didn't want to be a housewife. Eventually we devised a way to share household responsibilities.

We have been living together, happily for almost ten years now. I have no regrets about cohabitation. We frequently discuss getting married. I am in no rush, we are as good as married in our hearts, things are really great as they are, and I don't see any reason to make any changes now.

If your live-in relationship isn't working, consider it a blessing that you found out before getting married! Living together gives you a taste of who your partner really is. Most people behave differently at home compared to their behavior in public. You will really learn about the hygiene, and responsibility of your partner.

The true test of a relationship is living together. You will learn more about one another through daily interaction.

Caitlin Jones, Chicago, Illinois - Whether or not a live-in relationship would work depends entirely upon the couple in question. A person with religious / moral convictions would be quick to cite reasons and examples why a live-in relationship would not work, however one must understand their opinion is not objective, and may not be the best source of information for a decision.

The most famous argument against living-in with your significant other is that he or she would then be reluctant to take the next step into marriage. After all, who would want to buy the cow if the milk is free? Personally I find this argument silly like many others do. I, for sure, would not want someone to buy me just for my 'milk', and then decide to go through a costly divorce after they have drunk their fill. A live-in relationship would be a test of that. It is wise to see whether there is more than just an element of lust to the relationship.

Furthermore, it is crucial before a marriage to determine whether you and your mate are truly compatible. That includes seeing what it would be like to wake up to their quirks and habits and open toilet seats every morning. If there is no way to successfully cohabitate with your lover, better to know now than before an expensive "I do".

Furthermore, we must determine the definition of 'work'. While a life-long, marriage-less relationship would have been taboo back in the days, more and more couples are more comfortable considering themselves together without a piece of paper saying 'you did' and enough debt to feed a small country. Some would prefer to leave marriage in the back of their mind rather than rush into a legally binding agreement, which is wise as well considering the divorce rate.

In this day and age, with the divorce rate rising, it is wise to consider all angles and possibilities of a relationship before leaping into the married life. If a live-in relationship did not work...then it just did not work, like with the several people you dated in the past, it more than likely had nothing to do with the fact you lived with them. Furthermore, if you can expect a live-in relationship to not work, then how can one realistically expect a marriage to work?

One does not need to worry about failure if they decide to live with the one they love. They have nothing to lose, and everything, including wisdom, and insight to gain. After all, it is best to test the waters before leaping in.

Cyndi Haltom, Singapore – Live-in relationships are by far the best way to get to know another person especially in this over populated, under-educated world we live in today. Most people don't have the time to get to know someone outside of the home and therefore they must rely on the amount of time they have together and with work and other outside influences there isn't much time.

Living with someone allows each person to fully see all the faults of the other. Does he throw his dirty clothes on the floor knowing you'll pick them up which you do without a word but you hate it? Does he continuously come home late without calling and you say nothing because "at least he's here"? Does he refuse to help with the housework or shopping because he is a "man"?

And does she a listener or a gabber? Does she have self respect about her appearance, her home and lifestyle? Does she share the responsibilities of the expenses or is it his entire job because he "makes more money" or she "thinks he should support her"?

All these questions can be discovered before a person is getting married but it takes time and I can't see any other way than to live together and getting to know one another. People are so different in the way they are brought up, taught, their beliefs, in the way they like things done, how their relationship grows. All of these tests must be brought out into the open, discussed and realised. If they are not then divorce comes quickly because you find you have nothing in common with the one you have chosen.

I can't say everyone should live together but I do believe that unless you know the person you are going to spend the rest of your life with and unless it is tried and true it will be more difficult to understand them when you do come together. So I say try it, if you don't like it then try something else. There is no judgement worse than the one we place upon ourselves.

Lilith Russel, Carlow, Ireland – Although in some cultures and religions living together before marriage is just against the rules. Some people even call it "shacking up" or "Playing house". As horrid as these terms are, living together before marriage has its benefits. One of the benefits is to know each others' habits. You already know the good, the bad, and the ugly. Therefore when it comes down to living together after marriage the ghastly horror of knowing what she looks like before make-up won't send you into cardiac arrest.

If you live with your significant other, you may find yourself waking up very grumpy because they set the alarm for 6:30 a.m., hit snooze a couple of times, reset the alarm for later, then hit snooze again. All of this when you don't have to get up that morning at all and were hoping to sleep in! If you could just go back to living alone you'd never have this problem!

Does this make you angry all day? Or are you able to get over it and kiss them happily goodbye as they leave for work?

Each couple has a different dynamic with each other, and some are able to have great live-in relationships while others have less success. If within your relationship you can have your grumpy times, yet still be supportive of each other through them, you will be more likely to have a successful live-in relationship.

Living together means seeing each other at your best and at your worst. It takes patience, understanding, and a true level of caring for each other and love and respect of each other's company. It's up to each individual as well as each couple together to figure out if and how they can make a live-in relationship work - there are no absolutes when it comes to doing so. As with so many things, knowledge and awareness can help you on your journey to a good live-in relationship.

Just keep in mind - if it 'DOES' work, the best feeling in the world is when you get past that grumpiness in the morning and get to enjoy starting each day truly happy with someone you love, with good conversation, and with a kiss goodbye that makes your heart melt.

Hector Guzman, Poza Rica, Mexico - In my opinion, live-in-relationships are the only one that does work. With society the way it is now "TRUST" is at an all-time, record breaking low. Significant others have no faith in their counterparts. However, there are a few conditions that have to be met in order for the relationship to even get that far to begin with.

If you're gonna move in with a significant other you should love them. Sounds easy enough, right? Wrong! You need to be able to tolerate this person despite any annoying habits or character defects which may be discovered after you move in with them. I'm sure most of us have moved in with friends to discover that you can't stand living with them because they do this or that and it pisses you off. So, one need to be so in love with their significant other to know that no matter what they do you won't find yourself getting fed up with them down the line. You'll know this deep down in your heart; if you have to think about it and seriously debate it with yourself you may not be ready for such a big decision. You should also have not cheated on them, which will only lead to complications down the line. You'll either think that you now have free reign so you can get away with it over and over or your conscience will eat at you, rather subliminally and your feelings for your other will change. If you have cheated it'll catch up with you in one form or another. Then there will be a big mess as they move out, take most of your crap with them, and your stranded with their half the rent. There's more but this could seriously go on forever. Everyone's different, so the best advice is to just weigh the options carefully.

Maintaining this living situation is the true obstacle of the whole ordeal. You will fight. There will be fights, whether it's over that smeared lipstick on your collar from last night, which you can't really hide as she's waiting at the door for you to come home, or that she always leaves her tampons out in plain sight in the bathroom. Manage time spent together carefully. The couple cannot spend every waking moment of free time in the presence of the other. Set nights aside for personal time, go out with friends. If you didn't trust each other that much in the first place you shouldn't have moved in together.

You must also do things together. Go shopping. As much as we might deny it guys really do like to shop. Whether it be for clothing, food, movies or just window shopping. Like the advice your friends would give you would be much better? Be honest. Though difficult, yet necessary. Lying leads to nothing but the worst. Be open. If you're afraid to be yourself all the time there was no point in dragging a relationship out this far. Sometimes one partner just wants to make the other partner happy and so goes along with the stronger opinion denying their own. That is a recipe for disaster. Each person grew up with values and beliefs of some kind and should take them into honest account before entering into a live-in relationship. There's a lot that needs to be done to keep this relationship going, but you just need to feel out your loved one. The most important thing is the time apart though. It'll keep you from getting sick of each other and that's really what kills most relationships.

So, good luck! Living with your significant other is a huge step and a very rewarding one as well. Just work at it. If it's not working don't prolong it longer than it needs to be. It'll only be more damaging in the end. Life goes on. Don't be afraid.

Few Say "NO"

Imaad Ali, Bahowal, Pakistan - It seems to be a common misconception that living together prepares you for marriage.

Some argue that you will know the person you plan to marry better if you live with them first.

Or that you need to know if that person is sexually compatible, so why not try them out.

Still others believe that combining your money will help you save enough to get married.

I'm sorry to break this to you, but after marriage everything you thought you knew goes out of the window.

The guy or gal that rushed home every night to see you suddenly can't wait for a night out with friends.

Sex becomes a bargaining tool, or it becomes nonexistent.

And all the money you saved to get married and buy a home is usually spent carelessly on the honeymoon or a big screen TV (so you friends can come over since you're not allowed out anymore).

All the really good, sexually charged, and successful long lasting and financially settled marriages, started out with a young, inexperienced, and struggling couple.

This does not mean, shot gun "I'm pregnant" weddings.

To have a really successful marriage straight or gay, you need family support. And most families prefer to give support to a relationship that starts with commitment.

Tee Marie, Carolina, USA - Going against popular opinion living together is not a commitment it is merely playing house. Forgetting the spiritual implications of living in sin, (having sex before marriage) let's look at it as common sense.

When you are living with someone you can leave whenever you want, there is nothing holding you there. People break leases everyday if your name is even on it. Most men live in the woman's dwelling. Everyone has their role, cooking, cleaning, splitting the bills, but you are only there because you want to be. When things get tough, you happen to be out and meet someone else or you simply get bored, there's the door.

The big myth is we can live together and see how it will be when we're married. Sorry but it really is different. You are roommates trying to pass off a living arrangement for a spiritual union (and the two shall be as one).

I was raised in a religious home (went to church but no real relationship with God). I knew my parents weren't going to approve, but I was grown and me and my boyfriend of 3 years decided we were going to live together. We moved into a nice duplex on the bottom floor and our adventure began.

We both, went off to work, split the bills and went food shopping together. It was really no different than dating we were just under the same roof. There was no real talk of the future, just day to day living. I had my friends over, he had his. He got phone calls from female friends, no big deal because I knew if anyone crossed the line I could just pack up my things and go. We went along like this for a few months when he accidentally banged up the garage fixing the brakes on his friend's car.

His name wasn't on the lease so the landlord said I could stay but he had to go. Well we all know how that went over.

I went back to my parent's house and him to his grandmother's. We continued to date. Years later we did get married, and I can tell you there is a big difference having sex the way God intended without the guilt. I can't explain but you really do feel like one, you are part of that person and he is part of you - your best friend.

I can no longer run to my parents whenever we have and argument - they're not hearing it - and just pack up and leave. I made a commitment before God and man that we would stay together no matter what. If for someone reason there was something we couldn't get past, you still need to get legally separated or divorced you can't just walk away. Not to mention splitting all of your belongings.

Remember what your mom always told you about him not buying the cow when you can get the milk for free. This is really true. It took us 8 years to finally get married. There's nothing like the real thing, don't settle for a counterfeit.

Dima, Abaza - Wherever we go these days we hear the concept of live-in relationships, which is basically two people living together before marriage. A live-in relationship is almost like marriage, with a few exceptions. You need not file a divorce in case you decide to go your separate ways; you are not financially dependent on your partner, etc, etc. However, as you start living with each other 24 X 7, slowly and gradually expectations start cropping up.

You start demanding a lot from your partner, just like it happens in case of a marriage. You want to know where he / she is going, when he / she will be back to home and so on. Most of the people going in for a live-in relationship are those who are afraid of committing and who don't want the responsibilities that come along with being committed. They want the security of a relationship as well as the freedom and independence that comes with being a bachelor / spinster.

As an answer to the question that "do live-in relationships work", we can only say that the concept looks good for some time. However, after a certain period you feel the need for security and commitment. Also, marriage is any day better than a live-in relationship as sooner or later we all need somebody on whom we can fall back. And the surety that somebody will always be there for you can come only with commitment and with marriage.

Zochhuaka Hmar, Mizoram, India - Couples into a live-in relationship are more likely to split up that those who are tied into the holy matrimony. The data from the Office for National Statistics has also proves this fact.

Nearly, four-fifths of spouses who were married in 1991 are still living together, compared to three-fifths of cohabiting couples, who had a split up after barely five years.

Older couples and those with children were more likely to stay in the same relationship.

They found that out of those who were cohabiting in 1991, 61 percent were with the same partner for 10 years, while 39 percent were not. Of those who stayed together, most had by then married their partner. The majority whose relationship had ended were living alone.

In contrast to this, 82 percent of those who were married in 1991 were still living with their spouse till 2001. Of the 18 percent who had divorced or been widowed, most were single although a small proportion had remarried.

Therefore, it is evident that marriages are more stable than cohabitation.

Experts suggest that couples were more likely to split up if they were younger, had no children, had previously split up with their ex-partners, were poorly educated or were unemployed.

Living together can never be equivalent to marriage as far as family stability is concerned. To respect relationships, and have a secure family base, it is important to protect and support the institution of marriage.

Undeterred by social opinion, many couples prefer to live together before marriage, as they believe it is a precursor to any lifelong commitment. Still, a research by 'USA Today' suggests that some couples who cohabitate are not as happy as married couples.

It has been found, that the couples who lived together before marriage had a higher rate of divorce than those who did not lived-in. It is felt that the persons who lived together before marriage had lower levels of marital satisfaction (as all the social, emotional and physical pleasures are enjoyed beforehand) than those who did not live together. It has also been observed that the couples who have lived-in before marriage had more negative communication in their marriages than those who did not live together.

Gynnie Ann De Jesus, London, U.K. - I am trying not to be spiritualistic with this kind of relationship because it is talking about pre-marital relationship, which is primarily a sin; secondly it is much more convenient in the present days world, where the attitude is of use and throw. However, having a look at it in the superficial level, we get to know each other as time passes by. We can understand the depth of the relationship pertaining to tolerance, originality, adjustments and all the rest because we want to live together for the rest of our lives.

The best thing that two people can have in a relationship is, understanding. Understanding gives birth to all of the other aspects of a solid relationship. Understanding comes with time. If two people really take the time to get to know and trust each other. Than yes 'a live-in relationship can work'.

But realise that moving in with each other means that all of your little quarks are out in the open. All of those silly little things, that you do when you are all alone now become known to your partner.

The common purpose of any relationship must be growth. Everything around us must grow, including relationship. Without the common goal of growth, moving in together can strain a relationship.

Balance is another issue with living together. We can find it hard enough to balancing our own lifestyle. Now after moving in together you have to balance the life style of your partner as well. It is great to come home to someone who loves you. But living with the wrong person can cause you to hate to come home.

So make sure that your lifestyles are compatible, make sure that you have spent plenty of time getting to understand the person, that you are thinking about moving in with. Realise the sacrifice of space and privacy that you will be giving up. Ask yourself if you are ready to make that sacrifice. You have to overlook the broken fence in order to admire the beauty of the garden. Then you can make an educated decision about moving in together.

12

Why Do People Marry after a Long Live-In Relationship?

Marriage is still considered sacred, as it is in-built into our upbringing and couples, who are in long-term relationships want to be married before conception.

Live-in relationships may definitely more glamorous and easy, but marriage has its advantages as well. The Department of Economics at the University of Warwick in England carried out a study of 9,704 married people at the university in 2005. The study revealed that married people were deriving happiness from each other's happiness unlike those who were just living together. The research also indicated that marriage encouraged the habit of sharing among spouses, who stood by each other in both good and bad times.

Couples may live together without marriage but even in their hearts most of them believe that 'Marriage' is a pure and a loving relation between a man and a woman which is recognised by the society and the law. It is a relation in which they promise to "live together during the good or bad times, during richness and poverty, misery and health until death parts them". Well, all this seems to be very easy but it is in fact not easy to lead a happy, contented and a peaceful married life. There are situations where both, man and woman need to compromise and sustain their feelings to live a harmonious life. There should be a great understanding amongst the couple and they should be mentally compatible to face all the walks of life. For the younger generation, its love that exists in marriage and if there is no love between the couple, the marriage dissolves, but for older generation, the fact is different. It is not only love that builds the relation but other strong factors like understanding, concern, devotion and dedication towards each other which makes marriage a successful marriage. Getting a right person is not enough. You, yourself also have to be a right person.

There are some important reasons why people get married

1. To love and for being loved: A lot of people tie a knot because they are madly in love with each other. Marriage gives you a certificate to intensely and passionately love each other legally. There are no bounds to the extent of love. There is no thought of guilt as you are stamped as a married couple. This way you can shower love on your partner and be loved by your partner freely. Marriage fills up the loneliness in hearts of people longing for love (with no strings attached).

2. To protect and be cared for: Often People have a protection shield around them, especially females, once married. Women are at a greater risk when single, of being robbed, raped, teased etc. Once a woman gets married she feels secure in the arms of her man. Men on the other hand, feel wanted and they like the fact of being superior as they shelter a woman.

3. For Satisfaction, Pleasure and Security: A lot of people feel complete on getting married. They are satisfied and enjoy pleasures of life mentally, physically and sexually. There is a feeling of security amongst both partners mentally and financially, where both the partners can share their assets during difficult financial conditions.

4. Socially recognised and produce children legally: There are a lot of social pressures if you remain unmarried for quite a long time. Once married, people tend to respect you and tend to see you as a family oriented person. They term you as settled, once you are married. You can produce children and lead a typical family life with respect and love from your family as well as society.

5. To share responsibilities: Any person in this society is loaded with a lot of responsibilities where he / she cannot take it on his/her shoulders alone, so he / she needs a partner with whom he / she can share all his / her physical and mental responsibilities.

A case in point would be Meera Ahuja, an HR professional, who recently married after living in for a while. Sharing her insight, she says, "We were going out for two years before we decided to move in together. It definitely gave me a chance to know what I was getting into. It's different when you are dating and stay over at each other's place compared to when you are living together where you share everything from chores to bills. Living together isn't commitment with an escape hatch, as often noted by detractors. It is merely about questioning whether one can live and respect her partner for the rest of her life, instead of living a marriage that is purely perfunctory and meets social standards."

She adds, "They say the first year of marriage is the hardest and if you survive that, then you are in for a long haul. We already lived that. I never feel trapped that we have to be together now that we are married, but felt that I was given a chance to know him before I took the decision of living with him for the rest of my life."

Pamel Johnson Welsh, Lotschental Valley, Switzerland - In the case of me and my newlywed husband, of two and a half months, I can tell you our reasons. At first let me inform you that we lived together for several years. Both of us had been married previously, had children, and divorced each twice before we ever met one another. All of our children are grown, living away from home, with their own families. Therefore, we found it a considering factor that we live together, for a long time, before we ever considered committing to marriage again. This was agreeable to both of us from the very beginning as neither wanted to rush into marriage.

Living together allowed us time to experience one another. It also, gave us opportunities to grow and travel together.

We explored one another's differences and what habits we disliked about the other. We learned how we could live with them in a way that was accepting without putting a lot of strain on our relationship. In this way we felt we weren't changing the person whom we loved. For the last year we lived together we told everyone we were "life partners". We had already decided to be together for the rest of our lives at that point.

When you love someone so dearly, you realise you want to be there in many ways, especially in the final stages of life. As we are a middle-aged couple and there are some health issues on the table. This was one factor we considered. Even though, we were "life partners" that still is not recognisable legally in society unless "life partner" means "spouse". Therefore, in the event that one of us ended up in ICU, at the hospital, the other would not be able to visit. ICU will only allow family members. The other part of the health issue was insurance. My new husband has 'Multiple Sclerosis' (MS) and his shot therapy wasn't working. There was another option available. However, it would cost $5,000 per treatment. The treatment is once per month for the rest of his life if it is effective. Being that his MS is getting a bit worse meant he might not work much longer and would lose his only health insurance. I have a better health insurance plan, than the one his company offers, and it would be a benefit also when we got married.

Commitment was another factor. Not because neither of us had any issues surrounding insecurity. We had already committed to one another as "life partners" and the Christmas before he bought me a "couples ring" which had our birthstones and our names were engraved on it. I wore this ring on my left ring finger to signify my commitment to him and to others. It was more in a way of letting our families and others realise the depth of our commitment. Many felt, I believe, that I would not stay with Russ as his MS progressed. My husband had a wife leave him for this very reason. So I do understand their concerns. I have been in the Medical field off and on for about twenty-five years. I took care of my mother and grandmother when they were disabled also. I know what it takes and am up to do it for the ones I love. I felt committed to show my commitment in this way.

Above all, Love is the main reason everyone marries. It was no less the reason we did. When most people fall in love, sometimes it is fleeting; later to learn it was really lust. Therefore, to wait a long length of time is justified. You know for sure who you are marrying, that you really are in love and you can stand living with that person also. Those are great benefits to help you be sure your marriage is a successful one.

Krystle Hernandez (Fashion Designer), Modena, Italy - Marriage is many times better than the silly concept of 'live-in relationship', and even most of the people who live together without marriage have 'marriage' on their minds for the stability in life. Live-in sort of living only leads to the uncertainty and the couple is always doubtful whether at the end of the day the partner will come back home to stay or just to pick up the baggage and say goodbye for good.

And if lifelong marriage is your goal, as it is for the majorities of male-female couples who move in together, here are my ten recommendations for how to increase the chances that your marriage will be a success.

(1) Make the decision to live with a partner slowly, seriously, and with great care.

(2) Before you move-in together, be very clear about what you expect. You should both have a clear sense of what moving-in together means to each of you.

(3) Keep your expectations reasonable. Living together will not magically transform an "I'll never get married" guy into one who proposes on one knee. Sharing a kitchen and bedroom will not sweeten a volatile relationship. Live together because your relationship is going well, not to try to make it better.

(4) Similarly, do not marry your partner because you hope marriage will change him/her. If you do not like what you see in an unmarried significant other, you definitely will not like it in a spouse.

(5) Define the amount of time you want to live-in together. One way is to get engaged and set a wedding date before you move in together. Another possibility is to set a future date (six months or one year) at which time you both promise to have another serious conversation about marriage and make a definite decision about it.

(6) Write and sign a "living together agreement" to help clarify your expectations and define how you will handle finances and property. The conversations you will need to have in order to done this will strengthen your relationship and protect you later if you decide it is best to go your separate ways.

(7) Take couple education classes together. Research suggests that all couples have the same number of conflicts, but some handle conflicts well while others break up as a result of them. Couples' classes, which teach how to make sure your relationship can survive conflict, are often targeted for married or engaged couples. Before you sign up, make sure they believe in strengthening cohabits' relationships, too.

(8) If you are considering or planning to get married, talk about what will change and what things will stay the same.

(9) Use birth control. It is a lot more fun and romantic to get married because you want to, not because you accidentally got pregnant. The unplanned pregnancy rate is high among cohabits, but kids do best when they are wanted and planned. Whether you are married or not when you become a parent, your family will be strongest if it is fully intentional.

(10) Talk about marriage with people you respect who have been married a long time. Ask them about the hardest times, how and why they stayed together, what it was like when the relationship felt rocky, how they feel about it now.

The insights from long marriages can be inspiring and a good reality check.

Peggy Molloy, Bangkok, Thailand - Statistics bear up to the notion that when people live together, they very often will split up relatively soon once they are married. There are no guarantees with humans.

We use a different set of criteria for marriage, usually higher, than we do for dating, which can lead to the sexual-convenience and help-with-rent factors, involved with living together.

The person we need to love is ourselves. The effort we need to put forth in our relationships with others is our best, especially those we have sexual encounters with.

I will not live with a man (I'm a heterosexual femme) unless we are married. I will date, I will engage in intimacy if I believe I can trust him to be honest with me, and we are in a monogamous relationship, but I will not do his laundry, take phone messages from his mother, or shop for the groceries. How many times does the woman not only offer sexual services, but household chores as well...There is an open market for such tasks you know, and if he won't get you a ring, and marry you, then my friend, you are being underpaid, underemployed and disrespected.

If you hit the sack too soon, all the other multiple ways people need to relate well to one another for a successful marriage, hit the garbage bag.

I have no advice for anyone because I have made so many mistakes, and I have learned the traditional methods for marriage, dating and intimacy are more important than my generation from the sixties, had wanted to comprehend. We threw out the baby with the bath water **I'm afraid**, and **there aren't enough self-help books on the market to change all the societal damage done**. Example: if I had had a yearlong engagement period, I could have saved myself six years of a very unhappy marriage. I would have learned in that year, this person cannot possibly live up to my standards for a mate. No, I will not lower my standards to "have a man"....

The very least we can do is set an example by how we live our own lives now, and discuss these situations with women who might want to hear us. Our popular culture is woefully dedicated to dummying us down, so I urge caution when watching our media regarding how to manage or "un-manage" our personal relationships, friendships, and work situations. Most importantly, do not allow your intuition and self-respect to be undermined. Better to marry than to offer (sex and services) yourself for free.

Bruce McDaniel, Texas - Family pressures are one of the more common reasons. We are still in the age of the old school way of thinking. You know if you are not married (of course wishfully) you are living in sin. Thank goodness that is leaving the new age and way of thinking. Most people that live together for awhile finally decide they have found their partner. And decide to tie the knot. Some do it because they figure that the relationship has grown, and to the point that it is going to last forever.

Love is funny that way, and we cannot predict the future. There could be a pregnancy involved, an inheritance or maybe just the feelings that it is time to commit.

Speaking from experience, there are many factors involved and no one but the couple know the reasons why the decision was made.

My first wife and I lived together for eight months before we got married. This was due to us being in love and the family pressure we got married. A month after we got married we found out that she was pregnant, so this time it seemed legit. Wrong! We should have lived together longer as we divorced after one year.

The second wife and I got married after living together for nine months, everything was great until the family got involved and we divorced. Wait, we kept living with one another and got along great. Two years went by and we were still together and decided to try it again. Divorced again after six months but remained together again as a couple. The third bout of living together lasted three years. We would probably still be together if I had not got a promotion and moved out of state. She chose not to follow as if she remained she would inherit her daddy's land. We were together for seven years.

The third woman and fourth marriage for me was really family pressure. We lived with her mother from day one for nine months and pressures from her family caused us to tie the knot. Well, once again the failure of marriage, we divorced after four an half years.

My current and fifth marriage we knew from the day we met that we would get married some day. But we moved in together as roommates sharing expenses and social togetherness, as well romance. This was as we were waiting on the final divorce decree.

We got married after living together twenty months. We are soul mates, and just recently celebrated our One year anniversary.

People get married after a long live-in relationship as they believe they have found the one that they will be with the rest of their life! So, why do they? There are many reasons and like I said the couple has their own...maybe will never be divulged to anyone else.

13
Post Script

One day, Plato asked his teacher, "What is love? How can I find it?"

His teacher answered, "There is a vast wheat field in front. Walk forward without turning back, and pick only one stalk. If you find the most magnificent stalk, then you have found love."

Plato walked forward, and before long, he returned with empty hands having picked nothing.

His teacher asked, "Why did you not pick any stalk?"

Plato answered, "Because I could only pick once, and yet I could not turn back. I did find the most magnificent stalk, but did not know if there were any better ones ahead, so I did not pick it. As I walked further, the stalks that I saw were not as good as the earlier one, so I did not pick any in the end.

His teacher then said, "And that is love."

On another day, Plato asked his teacher, "What is marriage? How can I find it?

His teacher answered, "There is a thriving forest in front. Walk forward without turning back, and chop down only one tree. If you find the tallest tree, then you have found marriage."

Plato walked forward, and before long, he returned with a tree. The tree was not thriving, and it was not tall either. It was an ordinary tree. His teacher asked, "Why did you chop down such an ordinary tree?"

Plato answered, "Because of my previous experience. I walked halfway through the forest, but returned with empty hands. This time, I saw this tree, and I felt that it was not bad, so I chopped it down and brought it back. I did not want to miss the opportunity."

His teacher then said, "And that is marriage."

Once again our gay, lesbian, bisexual, and transgender neighbors are being forced to travel to the well at noon to get their water, when they can avoid the stares and sideways glances and whispers about who they are and how they live. They need brothers and sisters who will engage them in honest, loving relationships. They need people who will stand with them, accepting them with dignity and respect, accepting the gifts they have to offer. They need a word of hope, affirmation and grace.

In a much awaited observation on live-in relationships, the Honourable Supreme Court of India opined that a man and a woman living together without marriage cannot be construed as an offence. The Supreme Court said that there was no law prohibiting live-in relationships or pre-marital sex. "Living together is a right to live" the Supreme Court said, apparently referring to Article 21 of the Constitution of India which guarantees right to life and personal liberty as a fundamental right.

Live-in relation i.e. cohabitation is an arrangement whereby two people decide to live together on a long-term or permanent basis in an emotionally and / or sexually intimate relationship. The term is most frequently applied to couples who are not married.

In India, cohabitation had been a taboo since British rule. However, this is no longer true in big cities, but is still often found in rural areas with more conservative values. Female live-in partners have economic rights under Protections of Women and Domestic Violence Act, 2005.

The Maharashtra Government in October 2008 approved a proposal suggesting that a woman involved in a live-in relationship for a 'reasonable period' should get the status of a wife. Whether a period is a 'reasonable period' or not is determined by the facts and circumstances of each case.

The National Commission for Women (NCW) recommended to the Ministry of Women and Child Development that the definition of 'wife' as described in section 125 of Criminal Procedure Code must include women involved in a live-in relationship. The aim of the recommendation was to harmonise the provisions of law dealing with protection of women from domestic violence and also to put a live-in couple's relationship at par with that of a legally married couple. There was a Committee set up by the Supreme Court for this purpose, called the Justice Malimath Committee, which observed that "if a man and a woman are living together as husband and wife for a reasonably long period, the man shall be deemed to have married the woman."

The Malimath Committee had also suggested that the word 'wife' under Criminal Procedure Code be amended to include a 'woman living with the man like his wife' so that even a woman having a live-in relationship with a man would also be entitled to alimony. In a case, the Supreme Court observed that it is not necessary for a woman to strictly establish the marriage, to claim maintenance under section 125 of Criminal Procedure Code. A woman in a live-in relationship may also claim maintenance under section 125 Criminal Procedure Code.

In the case of Payal Katara vs. Superintendent, Nari Niketan Kandri Vihar Agra and Others, the Allahabad High Court ruled out that "a lady of about 21 years of age being a major has the right to live with a man even without getting married, if both so wish". The Supreme Court observed that a man and woman, if involved in a live-in relationship for a long period, they will be treated as a married couple and their child would be considered as legitimate.

The Supreme Court on an earlier occasion, while deciding a case involving the legitimacy of a child born out of wedlock has ruled, that if a man and a woman are involved in a live-in relationship for a long period, they will be treated as a married couple and their child would be legitimate. Also, the recent changes introduced in law through the Domestic Violence Act, 2005 gives protection to women involved in such relationships for a 'reasonable long period' and promises them the status of wives. A Supreme Court Bench headed by Justice Arijit Pasayat declared that children born out of such a relationship will no more be called illegitimate. "Law inclines in the interest of legitimacy and thumbs down 'whoreson' or 'fruit of adultery'."

The Supreme Court held that a child born out of a live-in relationship is not entitled to claim inheritance in Hindu ancestral coparcenary property (in the case of an undivided joint Hindu family) and can only claim a share in the parents' self-acquired property. The Bench set aside a Madras High Court judgment, which held that children born out of live-in relationships were entitled to a share in ancestral property as there was a presumption of marriage in view of the long relationship.

Reiterating an earlier ruling, a Vacation Bench of Justices B.S. Chauhan and Swatanter Kumar said, "In view of the legal fiction contained in Section 16 of the Hindu Marriage Act, 1955 (legitimacy of children of void and voidable marriages), the illegitimate children, for all practical purposes, including succession to the properties of their parents, have to be treated as legitimate. They cannot, however, succeed to the properties of any other relation on the basis of this rule, which in its operation, is limited to the properties of the parents."

A child can only make a claim on the person's self acquired property, in case the child is illegitimate. It can also be interpreted in a way in which a child could lay a claim on the share of a parents' ancestral property as they can ask for that parents' share in such property, as Section 16 permits a share in the parents' property. Hence, it could be argued that the person is not only entitled to self acquired property but also a share in the ancestral property.

The (Supreme) Court also stated that while the marriage exists, a spouse cannot claim the live-in relationship with some other person and seek inheritance for the children from the property of that other person. The relationship with some other person, while the husband is living is not 'live-in relationship' but 'adultery' (Bharatha Matha and Anr. vs. R.Vijaya Ranganathan and Others.) It is further clarified that 'live-in relationship' is permissible in unmarried heterosexuals (in case, one of the said persons is married, the man may be guilty of adultery and it would amount to an offence under Section 497 of the Indian Penal Code).

The law does not prescribe how we should live; it is ethics and social norms which explain the essence of living in welfare model. The Court itself notices that what law sees as no crime may still be immoral. It has said in a judgement of 2006, notices by the Court now, that two consenting adults engaging in sex is not an offence in law "even though it may be perceived as immoral." Of course, such protective sanctions may potentially lead to complications that could otherwise be avoided. But simply raising the hammer may not be the best route to taming the bold and the brave. This is not the first time live-in relationship is in the ambit of debates and discussions. There has been a long-standing controversy whether a relationship between a man and a woman living together without marriage can be recognised by law. With changing social hypothesis entering the society, in most places, it is legal for unmarried people to live together. Now even in a country like India bounded by innumerable cultural ethics and rites, the law finds legally nothing wrong in live-in relationships.

This, however, cannot be construed that law promotes such relationships. Law traditionally has been biased in favour of marriage. It reserves many rights and privileges to married persons to preserve and encourage the institution of marriage. Such stands, in particular cases of live-in relationship, it appears that, by and large, is based on the assumption that they are not between equals and therefore women must be protected by the courts from the patriarchal power that defines marriage, which covers these type of relationships too.

The Supreme Court of India on 21.10.2010 said a live-in relationship for purely sexual needs cannot make the partners eligible for the benefits of a marriage

The Supreme Court ruled that each and every live-in relationship could not be categorised as a "relationship in the nature of marriage" which entitles women to maintenance.

"If a man has a 'KEEP' whom he maintains financially, and uses mainly for sexual purpose and as a servant, it would not be a relationship in the nature of marriage," the court said delivering a judgement on a couple who lived together for 14 years.

A court in Tamil Nadu and the Madras High Court had ruled in favour of the woman who had demanded maintenance from the man when their relationship ended, but the male partner had challenged the verdict in the Supreme Court.

"Merely spending weekends together or a one-night stand would not make it a domestic relationship. In our opinion, not all live-in relationships will amount to a relationship in the nature of marriage to get the benefit of the Act of 2005. To get such benefits, the conditions mentioned by us must be satisfied, and this has to be proved by evidence," the Bench ruled. The court said whether the woman was a 'Mistress' or like a 'Wife' had to be ascertained first.

The Supreme Court said a woman in a live-in relationship is not entitled to maintenance unless she fulfilled the parameters of a marriage like relationship. "In our opinion a 'relationship in the nature of marriage' is akin to a common law marriage" recognised in some countries in the absence of a formal marriage, a Bench comprising Justices Markandey Katju and T. S. Thakur said.

The Bench acknowledged that its view would exclude many women who "have had a live-in relationship from the benefit of the 2005 Act, but then it is not for this Court to legislate or amend the law." "No doubt because of this view many women who had a live-in relationship would be excluded from the benefit of the provisions the protection of Women from Domestic Violence Act 2005, which talks about relationship in the nature of marriage" the Supreme Court said.

The Court took upon itself the trouble of laying down the conditions as Parliament while enacting the law in 2005 had used the expression "relationship in the nature of marriage" and not "live-in relationship," the Bench explained. Section 125 of Criminal Procedure Code provided for maintenance only to the legally-wedded wife, dependent parents and children. But the Domestic Violence Act expanded the scope to relationship "in the nature of marriage."

The Bench said it felt the need for interpreting it because a large number of cases of this nature would be coming up before various courts in the country. "In our opinion, Parliament by the aforesaid Act has drawn a distinction between the relationship of marriage and a relationship in the nature of marriage, and has provided that in either case the person who enters into either relationship is entitled to get the benefit of the Act."

Talking about the changes sweeping the society, the Bench said in feudal society sexual relationship between man and woman outside marriage was totally taboo and regarded with disgust and horror. This was depicted in Leo Tolstoy's novel "Anna Karenina," Gustave Flaubert's novel "Madame Bovary" and the novels of the great Bengali writer Sharat Chandra Chattopadhyaya.

"However, Indian society is changing, and this change has been reflected and recognised by Parliament" by enacting the law against domestic violence, the Apex (Supreme) Court opined.

The Bench laid down the definition in a case by a man challenging the claim of a woman that she was his wife. The bench said that in order to get maintenance, a woman in a live-in relationship must "hold themselves out to society as being akin to spouses and for significant period of time".

The basic parameters laid down for live-in couple are

(1) The couple must hold themselves out to society as being akin to spouses.

(2) They must be of legal age to get married.

(3) They must have voluntarily cohabited and held themselves out to the world as being akin to spouses for a 'significant period of time'. (The Bench underlined the words "for a significant period of time" without specifying any time period).

(4) The couple must have lived together in a "shared household", as defined in Section 2(s) of the Protection of Women from Domestic Violence Act, 2005 of Indian Penal Code.

Index